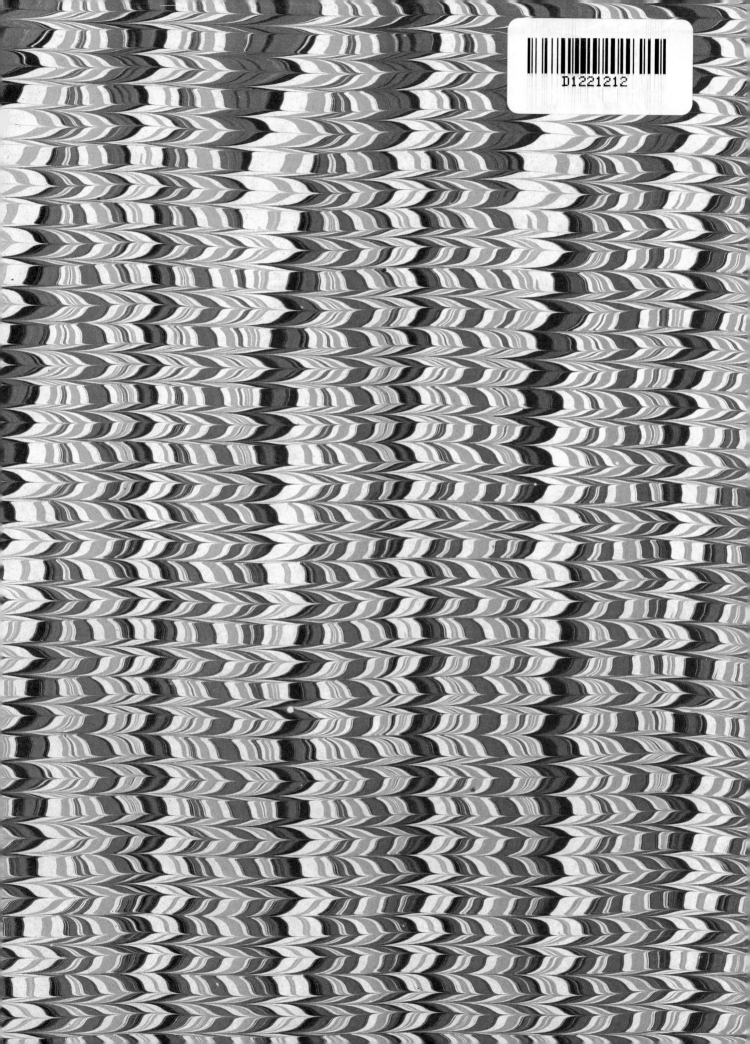

Szymanowski

ca 1922

Stanislaw Golachowski
*Translated from Polish to German by Henryk P. Anders; translated
from German to English by Christa Ahrens.*

ISBN 0-86622-014-3

© 1986 by Paganiniana Publications, Inc.

© by Polskie Wydawnictwo Muzyczne Kraków, Poland 1983

PAGANINIANA PUBLICATIONS, INC.
211 West Sylvania Avenue, Neptune City, New Jersey 07753

Contents

The Childhood Years

Karol Szymanowski at the age of 15.

A view of Timoshovka, Szymanowski's birthplace.

Szymanowski's native country was the Ukraine. He was born on the 3rd of October, 1882, in Timoshovka, a village situated in the province of Kiev. At that time, part of Timoshovka actually belonged to the Szymanowski family, who ranked among Polish landowners of average wealth in the Ukraine. To all appearances, the environment in which Karol Szymanowski spent the years of his childhood and youth was in no way out of the ordinary. Neither the social standing nor the material situation enjoyed by his parents exceeded that of the average Polish landowner in the Ukraine at the turn of the century. It was a period of gradual decline for the Polish land-owning class in this region.

Like the other families, the Szymanowskis were affected by the inevitable historical development which ended in the 1917 October Revolution and the dispossession of the landlords. The Szymanowskis, however, raised themselves above their environment by the high standards they set themselves in their artistic pursuits. The wealth of musical talent among the Szymanowskis and their nearest relatives is truly unique. In the course of less than twenty years, the house of Szymanowski, in the middle of the Ukrainian steppes, became an oasis of a high musical culture such as one would search for in vain even in the musical centers of the great European metropolises.

Early indications of the Szymanowski family's future blossoming in the realm of music were already to be found in the composer's parents. Stanislaw Korwin-Szymanowski, Karol's father, whom circumstances prevented from pursuing to its full potential his natural talent for the exact sciences, was eminently musical. It was to him that Karol and his siblings owed the fact that, from the very beginning, their musical education was based on the best traditions of European music. Only the works of great musicians – with Mozart and Beethoven taking pride of place – appeared on the Szymanowskis' piano, sometimes in a simplified version adapted to the modest accomplishments of young musical adepts.

Perhaps it was too strict and rigorous a musical education, but the teaching at this exactingly high level was rewarded by a corresponding degree of success; from the very first, it encouraged Karol's development in the field of music to proceed in the most favorable direction, since the boy had already been able to acquaint himself with all the best works in musical literature in his childhood. Piano lessons with this in mind were given consecutively to all the children in the family of Stanislaw and Anna (née Taube) Szymanowski – i.e., Anna, Feliks, Karol, Stanislawa, and Zofia. Three of them subsequently chose to become professional musicians: Feliks became a pianist, Karol a composer, and Stanislawa a singer.

The Szymanowskis were related to two families of almost equal musical talent, namely the Blumenfeld and the Neuhaus families. The Blumenfelds were originally from Bavaria, the Neuhauses had come to the Ukraine from the Rhineland. Among the Blumenfelds, Feliks was the most outstanding musician. During Karol's youth he had held important posts in the musical world of Russia, being not only a good pianist but also a notable conductor and composer. Among the works he composed were *24 Preludes* for piano, which were part of the permanent repertoire at the villa in Timoshovka. His brother Zygmunt was a singer and composer, the second brother – Stanislaw – a music teacher and proprietor of a school of music in Kiev. His sister Joanna was a singer and, finally, his second sister – Marta – a pianist.

Marta Blumenfeld had married the music teacher Gustaw Neuhaus with whom she jointly ran a school of music in Yelisavetgrad (now Kirovograd). This school was attended by every one of the Szymanowski children. The Neuhaus couple had two children who were of the same age as the young Szymanowskis: Harry (Heinrich) and Natalia; both were excellent pianists. Harry Neuhaus became one of the most outstanding piano tutors in the Soviet Union. Nor was there a shortage of musical talent on the maternal side of the composer's family – that is, among the Taubes.

These four families – Szymanowski, Blumenfeld, Neuhaus, and Taube – maintained very close relationships, and by their common efforts, as it were, created this unique "enclave" of great music: the House of Szymanowski.

During the early years of Karol's childhood the Szymanowskis lived in the village of Orlovka. They did not move to Timoshovka until after the grand-father, Feliks Szymanowski, had died. Generally, only the summer months were spent in Orlovka and – later – Timoshovka by the Szymanowski children. In the winter they lived in the small town of Yelisavetgrad, nearby, where the Szymanowskis owned two houses. In Yelisavetgrad the children attended the Neuhaus' school of music, and Feliks and Karol also went to the local secondary school.

Karol's childhood was not a happy one. In about his fourth year of life, he sustained a leg injury which deprived him of movement for several years, and then left him with a slight limp for the rest of his days. There can be no doubt that this disability cast a shadow over Karol's emotional life, since the way he spent his childhood of necessity had to differ from that of his fit and healthy contemporaries. For him, books and musical scores had to take the place of games and foolish pranks in the fields of Timoshovka.

Karol began to have regular music lessons when he was seven years old. At first these were given him by his father and later by his aunt Maria, who also initiated Karol's brothers and sisters into the rudimentaries of piano-playing. Finally, Karol was taught at the Neuhaus' school.

Also into the childhood years fall two musical events which remained with the composer until he died. Both were connected with opera. The first was that, at the small theater in Yelisavetgrad, he was able to hear the popular opera *Russalka* by Alexander Dargomizhsky, performed in all probability by some group of travelling musicians. The tremendous impression which this first contact with the magic world of opera made on the child – as recounted by the composer himself – fundamentally influenced him in the choice of his future career. The second great musical experience Karol had was Wagner's *Lohengrin*, which he heard in Vienna when stopping there with his parents on the way to Switzerland.

The Szymanowskis were heading to Geneva to sort out some problems in connection with an inheritance. The physician Oswald Szymanowski, who had lived there, had willed a villa with beautiful antique furniture and a collection of historical objects to the composer's father. Oswald Szymanowski was a descendant of the Napoleonic general Jozef Szymanowski. The Szymanowskis sold the villa while, however, removing the furniture and all historical mementos to Timoshovka. Karol returned from this journey with pianoforte arrangements of Wagner operas, and these sheets of music now became the object of his zealous study.

In his early years, Karol in no way stood out amongst the musically gifted children in the Szymanowski family. Whereas the older brother Feliks and the Neuhaus children already excelled in their mature ability on the piano, Karol lagged markedly behind them in this respect. Incidentally, he never became an outstanding pianist, although difficult circumstances later on were sometimes to

Karol Szymanowski's parents Stanislaw Korwin-Szymanowski and Anna Szymanowska, *nee* Taube.

6

**Karol Szymanowski and his sister
Zofia coming home from tennis
court.**

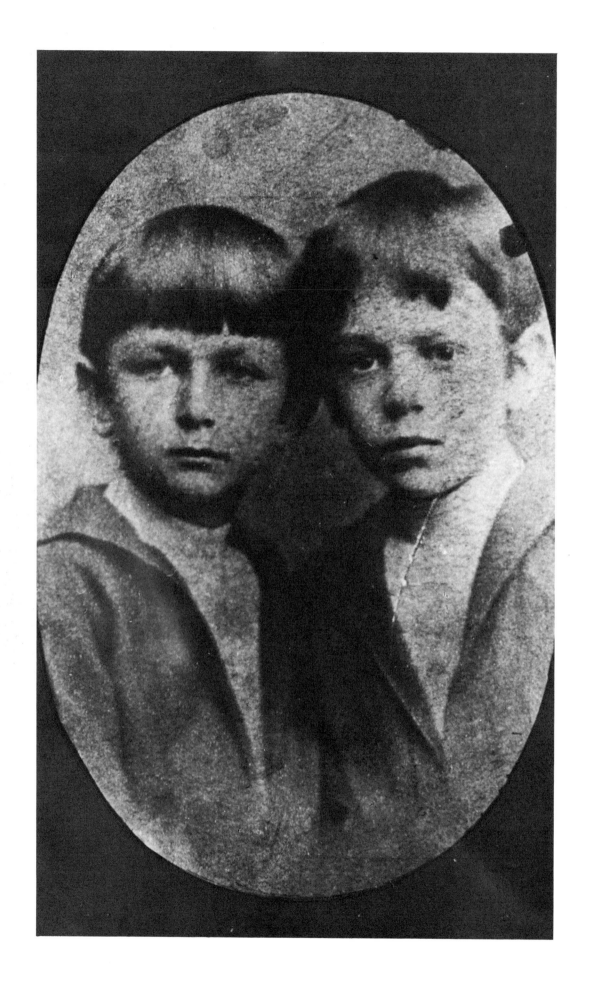

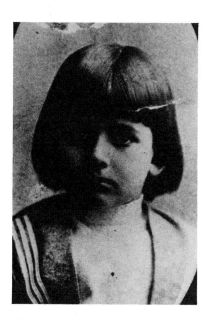

Stanislawa Szymanowska.

force him into adopting the role of concert virtuoso. On the other hand, there was no doubt about his creative ability. However, progress made in composing is not as immediately obvious to those around as is an improvement in piano-playing or singing.

To engage in the art of composition was, in fact, a common pursuit in the Szymanowski household. With a confidence characteristic for their age, the young composers got straight down to operas and operettas. These they wrote either by themselves or as a joint effort, and subsequently performed them in front of an audience formed by relatives and neighbors. Only two of these youthful operas have survived: *Golden Summit*, which was written by Karol alone, and *Roland*, which he composed jointly with his brother Feliks. The tradition of such improvised musical performances was still continuing in Timoshovka when Karol had already become a mature composer.

In his memoirs, Dr. Marceli Nalecz-Dobrowolski recounts his impressions of the Szymanowski House he gathered while staying there after 1906: "Almost every family get-together transformed the drawing-room at Timoshovka into a concert hall. Libretti and music for operettas were written on the spot, stage decor was quickly painted, and instant performances took place on an improvised stage. Another time, colorful sleigh-outings in costume were organised for everyone, or living pictures created to musical accompaniment. There was choral song, dancing, and declamation. Summer saw the zenith of the wide range of artistic performances in which Karol Rosciszewski—who owned the second part of Timoshovka—and his wife were also actively involved, as were a number of 'accidental' amateurs who had been recruited by neighbors and guests."

In addition to these childish operas Karol also wrote other works, unconsciously selecting such types of music as could be performed in the family circle, i.e., piano pieces and songs. However, none of his early creative efforts appears to have caused any great resonance among the members of his family. It was not until 1900 that Szymanowski had produced anything he later considered worthy of a permanent place in his oeuvre. These are already the compositions of a young man of eighteen years of age.

Facing page:
Karol and his brother Felix.

Szymanowski with family and
friends in 1903 in Elizavetgrad,
where he graduated from high
school in 1900.

Karol Szymanowski, age three.

A 1905 photo of Karol Szymanowski.

The knight's room, with an arms collection, in the Timoshovka house.

Szymanowski in 1910.

Student Years in Warsaw

Grzegorz Fitelberg.

In 1901 — after his period of study with Gustaw Neuhaus who instructed him in musical theory and piano-playing — Szymanowski went to Warsaw, where he started to study harmony and, later, composition under Marek Zawirski and Zygmunt Noskowski.

Szymanowski came to Warsaw under the guardianship of his uncle, Marcin Korwin-Szymanowski, who was the director of a mining company and came from Krivoy Rog in the Ukraine. Szymanowski enjoyed telling people about the first time he and his uncle called on Emil Mlynarski,† who was then the greatest living authority on music in Warsaw. Whilst expressing the highest praise for the pieces the young composer had played to him, Mlynarski — on learning of the latter's intention to devote his life entirely to music — then went on to point out all the problems and drawbacks a musician's life would bring. He thought it far better for a landowner's son to devote himself to agriculture instead of risking the uncertain fate of a composer. Composing, in his opinion, was a profession which seldom brought sufficient rewards. It gave Szymanowski great satisfaction that despite the warnings uttered by this prominent musician he had not been discouraged from his chosen path — that he had become a composer and was able to support himself fairly adequately by his creative work.

Szymanowski did not enroll at the Warsaw Conservatory but took private lessons with Zawinski and Noskowski. These studies lasted until 1905. Within a relatively short time he acquired the reputation of being Noskowski's best pupil. His work during this period concentrated mainly on mastering compositional technique.

A fellow student at Noskowski's, the well-known composer Ludomir Rozycki, writes in his "Remembrance of Szymanowski": "He was not able to work with bureaucratic regularity, but once he had started on a composition or a part of it, he could spend hours sitting over his music-paper in deep concentration, covering the whole sheet with minute notes. (. . .) When he was composing his piano sonata (the first), how often I found Szymanowski at the piano studying the structure of piano passages by Chopin and Scriabin with the utmost thoroughness! For him this music contained the secrets of piano style, and he knew how to unravel them. In fact, every one of his piano passages already possessed excellent pianistic qualities even at that time. When he showed me the music he had already composed, I was impressed both by the solidity and maturity of the structure and by the concentration of his invention."

Szymanowski used every opportunity to perfect his knowledge of the craft of composition. He zealously attended the rehearsals and concerts of the Warsaw Philharmonic Orchestra, where he learnt the difficult art of composing for orchestra. He made friends among important instrumentalists and carefully observed them in their daily work in order to get an all-around knowledge of the playing techniques on the different instruments. From the first years of his stay in Warsaw date his friendships with the conductor Grzegorz Fitelberg, the violinist Pawel Kochanski, and the pianist Arthur Rubinstein. All three of these artists played an important role in his life.

Szymanowski's creative work during his years of study in Warsaw developed

---

†Mlynarski was the director of the Warsaw Philharmonia founded in 1901.   13

mainly within the scope of what were then the composers he most admired: Chopin, Scriabin, Wagner, and Richard Strauss. This does not mean that he copied them slavishly. What he tried to do was to assimilate their technical achievements in composition and from this foundation to evolve his own musical language.

Already the works composed by Szymanowski in his youth clearly show a characteristic which was to become a feature of the majority of his best works: a strong emotional tension which sometimes intensifies into ecstasy. This ecstasy is probably the most tangible characteristic of Szymanowski's music and it was preserved even when the style of his compositions underwent radical changes.

This is because Szymanowski's experience of music was above all emotional. We can see this, for example, from the characteristic description he applied to musical works he liked. He almost never referred to a piece of music as "beautiful"; his term of praise was that it was "moving." Contrary to some hostile criticism in Poland, Szymanowski was never a calculating composer who planned the effects of his works in cold blood. Everything he ever composed he had first experienced on the deepest emotional level, even if he then perhaps transcribed it into a musical language which was not immediately comprehensible to everyone.

By the time Szymanowski came to Warsaw, he had already assembled a rich collection of his own compositions, notably works for the piano: numerous preludes and etudes, two sonatas (G minor and F sharp minor), drafts of variations, as well as the Sonata for Violin in E major, songs based on texts by Verlaine, Nietzsche, and Tetmajer, and the pianoforte arrangement of a musical drama—of unknown title—in Wagnerian style. Some of these—his earliest—works the composer considered worth printing and publishing. They were: *The Preludes*, op. 1, *Songs*, op. 2 (which were settings of poems by Tetmajer), and the *Four Etudes for Piano*, op. 4. During his studies with Noskowski the drafts of piano variations grew into two cycles, namely *Variations in B flat minor* op. 3 and the *Variations on a Polish Folk Theme in B minor*, op. 10.*

Among these works is one of the most popular compositions by Szymanowski: the Etude in B flat minor which Ignacy Paderewski included in his repertoire and thus made widely known. Oddly enough, Szymanowski was never very fond of any compositions of his which were particularly popular with audiences. The Etude in B flat minor was not one of his favorites either.

In a letter written to Grzegorz Fitelberg in 1910 Szymanowski stated, "During the banquet Paderewski introduced himself to Stasia.† He made various pleasant remarks to her about me, particularly of course in relation to the famous Etude in B flat minor, op. 4, no. 3. It is fatal to have composed one's 9th Symphony so young."

Much later, in a letter written to Anna Iwaszkiewicz†† in 1932, he explained this—to all appearances so curious—attitude in a little more detail: "You know how confused and vexing my feelings about my own music are. The liking a certain few people have for it gives me encouragement and fills me with joy. On the other hand, the fact that certain others like it makes me have doubts as to its value."

During his student years in Warsaw, Szymanowski found himself in an artistic environment which was highly conservative in its attitudes. Despite the fact that, like today, Warsaw was lying at the crossroads of main routes of Europe and the currents of cultural life had ready access to this city from all directions, its musical life was "deeply provincial" in Szymanowski's day. It was a time in which European music was totally dominated by the genius of Richard Wagner. All the young composers throughout Europe were under the spell of his works. Bayreuth, where the Wagner Festival took place each year, became the musical Mecca of Europe to which young musicians made their pilgrimage in order to experience the ecstasy of hearing *Tristan* and the *Ring des Nibelungen*. They succumbed not only to the magic of Wagner's musical drama but also to the artistic ideology he had proclaimed in numerous publications. Thus Karol

Pawel Kochanski, a violinist who was the first to perform Karol's violin pieces.

†Stasia was the singer Stanislawa Szymanowska, Karol's sister.
††She was the wife of the well-known poet Jaroslaw Iwaszkiewicz who was K. Szymanowski's cousin.

*See page 73 for music examples 1 and 2.

14

Szymanowski, too, went on pilgrimages to Bayreuth.

At that time no one could have foreseen the dangers that were inherent in the music of "the old magician from Bayreuth." Nor did anyone heed the warning uttered by the master himself in his esthetic works: " 'Beware!' I say to those that follow me." Wagner's artistic world – intoxicating because of the wealth and variety of musical and dramatic resources – suddenly seemed to open up entirely new vistas to European music. A new musical era appeared to have begun. Not until the years immediately preceding World War I was it finally recognized that Wagner's oeuvre had in fact marked the end of an epoch, that it had represented the climax of romantic music, and that it was impossible to continue to move in the same direction – just as it is impossible to climb any higher once the mountain summit has been reached. Meanwhile, however, the name Wagner was synonymous with musical progress, and "Wagneritis" – as it was generally called in conservative musical circles – was a form of musical obsession.

Warsaw had little time for Wagner and his musical heir Richard Strauss. Polish composers, then at the zenith of their creative maturity, looked to the sentimental Mendelssohn as the artistic ideal worthy of imitation. The revolutionary currents following in the wake of Wagner's music were upsetting the musical life all over Europe and the reaction of Polish musicians was one of terror. Describing the musical scene in Warsaw at that time, Henryk Opienski once refers to Wagner's *Tristan* as a myth the mere knowledge of which could inflict serious harm.

For a young composer whose head was brimming with new ideas it was difficult to gain a foothold in this environment. Anything outside the mold of classical music was strictly prohibited. The school of composition Szymanowski had to endure at Zygmunt Noskowski's must have seemed little less than torture to him.

Apart from Szymanowski, three other talented young composers stood out in the musical world of Warsaw at that time: Grzegorz Fitelberg, Ludomir Rozycki, and Apolinary Szeluto. These young musicians quickly made friends with each other. What they had in common were their progressive artistic attitudes. Furthermore, united, it was easier for them to go against the stuffy musical atmosphere that prevailed in the capital. Here there was scant opportunity for them to hear modern music or, as Wagner and his disciples called it, "music of the future." If they wanted works by Wagner and Strauss, they had to content themselves with playing passages from pianoforte arrangements.

In his *Remembrance of Szymanowski* already cited, Ludomir Rozycki describes such "revelries" at the piano as follows: "Our favorite pastime was to play Richard Strauss's symphonic poems with four hands. Particularly the finale from *Death and Transfiguration* we could play over and over again, with the piano booming and thundering in the process, to our intense delight – and then a prolonged period of silence so that nothing of the impact was lost."

The more the young composers progressed in their studies – and the number of new works in their music folders increased – the more they realized that their future as artists depended on their extrication from the Warsaw environment. Consequently they decided to overcome the usual obstacles put into the way of aspiring composers, by uniting their strength. Their first concern was to ensure that their works appeared in print and that a publisher could be found abroad, for if their compositions had been published in their native country, they would have been left lying on the bookshop shelves for years on end. As there was no reasonable hope of finding a publisher willing to take on the high cost of printing the works of totally unknown Polish composers, they decided to found their own publishing company. The most active among the four – Grzegorz Fitelberg – procured a wealthy patron who agreed to give financial backing to their enterprise. This patron was Prince Wladyslaw Lubomirski, a rich aristocrat who fancied himself a composer – an aspiration he could not have realized without con-

Richard Wagner.

siderable help from his tutor, who happened to be Fitelberg.

Funded by the Prince, a syndicate was formed in the fall of 1905 which bore the name "Spolka Nakladowa Mlodych Kompozytorow Polskich" (Publishing Syndicate of Young Polish Composers). Since the composers belonging to this association also represented the musical avant-garde of Poland, they became known as "Mloda Polska w muzyce" (Young Poland in Music) by analogy with the literary avant-garde of that time.

In the musical journal *Lutnista*, the young composers defined as follows the goals the publishing syndicate had set itself: "It is the aim of this association to promote modern Polish music through concerts and the publishing of members' own works. This, it is hoped, will enable members to go forward courageously in the pursuit of their artistic careers and help them to become largely self-reliant by freeing them from the—sometimes awkward—dependency on publishers on the one hand, and the various impresarios on the other."

Thanks to the Prince's generosity, the publishing company soon became a reality and Berlin was chosen for its location, inasmuch as the young composers were not concerned merely with having their works published but also wanted to introduce them to the musical world of Europe. In Berlin the business side of the association was represented by the publisher Albert Stahl, whose main concern was the retail sale of the published works. The first publications appeared already in 1905; they were works by Rozycki and Szeluto. Then, in 1906, the first printed copies of the Nine Preludes, op. 1, by Karol Szymanowski were released. They showed all music lovers and musicians that an unusual composer had come upon the scene of Polish music.

In the same year Szymanowski gave the first public performance of his works. On February 6th, 1906, the members of the "publishing syndicate" gave a concert at the Warsaw Philharmonia. This concert marked the beginning of an important process in Polish music which allowed it at long last to rise to the same level as European musical culture. At the afore-mentioned concert, the orchestra played (under the leadership of Grzegorz Fitelberg) the Concert Overture in E major, op. 12, and (under Harry Neuhaus) the Variations in B minor, op. 10, and the Etude in B flat minor by Szymanowski. The programme also included works by Fitelberg, Rozycki, and Szeluto, as well as a piece by the princely patron: his Andante for Orchestra. *

After the concert Aleksander Polinski, the most influential music critic in Warsaw, wrote in the *Kurier Warszawski*: "Listening to yesterday's performance of the works by Mr. Karol Szymanowski, I did not doubt for a moment that I was confronted here with a composer of outstanding merit if not of genius. For, everything he has created so far has been stamped with the mark of genius. In his Piano Variations on a Folk Theme as much as in his extraordinarily beautiful Etude in B flat minor—which Chopin himself might have claimed as his own—and in his Overture there is a wealth of beautiful melodies of unquestionable originality, of excellent-sounding harmonies, and the appropriately applied effects of a rich polyphony, and all these attractive components are transfigured by poetry and enlivened by youthful imagination, and the whole of this is joined together by a healthy guiding principle."

The reviews by other critics in Warsaw were generally written in a similar vein. Among the four gifted composers, it was Karol Szymanowski who was placed in the foreground by everyone. For the first time in his life, the young composer experienced a period of triumph for and general interest in his talent. But these happy hours were not to last for long. Already in the following year the same Polinski condemned Szymanowski and his colleagues. For the moment, however, "Young Poland in Music" had caused a sensation. The concert had to be repeated.

After the Warsaw concerts all four of the young composers travelled to Berlin, where Prince Wladyslaw Lubomirski organized a concert of their own works for

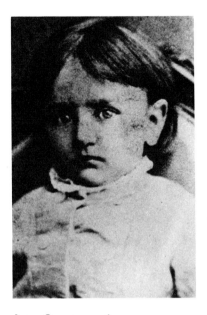

Anna Szymanowska.

   *See page 74 for music example 3.

his protégés. Once again the Warsaw programme was offered to the public. This concert took place on March 30th, 1906, in the Beethoven Hall with the excellent Berlin Philharmonic Orchestra under the leadership of Fitelberg. The debutants were given a friendly reception by the audience, which included a number of German musicians who had been attracted by the promise of novelties. If the audience's warmth was not echoed by the reviewers, then this was largely for political reasons. It was at that time that the "Hakatists" grew ever more influential and intensified their anti-Polish propaganda.

In Szymanowski's career as a composer, his contact with the musical world of Berlin—a city then still considered the musical capital of Europe—marked the end of his first creative period and a change of direction in his musical style. A total of fourteen opus numbers derive from that period. Among these, his songs are the most deserving of special mention, apart from the piano works already referred to.

From the earliest days of his musical creativity, Szymanowski had demonstrated a lyrical talent of the highest caliber. The deeply moving *Three Fragments from the Poetry of Jan Kasprowicz*, op. 5, "The Swan," op. 7 (words by Waclaw Berent), or at least "Lullaby for the Little Child Jesus," op. 13, no. 2 (settings of poems from *Des Knaben Wunderhorn*), and "Suleika" op. 13, no. 4 (text by Friedrich Bodenstedt) are true lyrical masterpieces. Such heights of inspiration as are shown in these songs were not reached by any other Polish composer of this epoch. *

Karol Szymanowski in Tunis in 1914.

*See pages 74-75 for music example 4 and pages 75-76 for music example 5.   17

Above: The founders of the "Young Poland" musical group: Karol Szymanowski, Apolinary Szelutko, Wladyslaw Lubomirski, Grzegorz Fitelberg, Ludomir Rozycki. *Below:* Karol Szymanowski, Heinrich Neuhaus and Michalina Przyszychowska in front of the composer's Timoshovka house in 1906.

Under the Spell of German Music

The drawing-room in Timoshovka.

In the years that followed, Szymanowski was greatly influenced by German music. Between 1906 and 1908, he made several trips to Berlin and Leipzig, where he familiarized himself with contemporary German music.

Apart from Richard Strauss and Wagner, whose major works he had already become acquainted with during his stay in Warsaw, it was above all the music of Max Reger which had a special influence on him.

The mainstream of German music at that time endeavored to continue within the framework of Wagner's musical style, generally choosing the path of least resistance. Instead of searching for the solution to new artistic problems which had not been exhaustively dealt with in Wagner's works, there was a tendency among composers to try and outshine both Wagner and one another in the employment of technical aids for their music. The powerful masses of sound from the orchestra which were in keeping with the special requirements of Wagnerian drama assumed well-nigh monstrous dimensions in the symphonic works of Richard Strauss. German composers of that time also tried to outdo Wagner in the concentration of harmony and by making the polyphonic interweaving of melodies ever more complicated.

Szymanowski, at this time, was still striving to become proficient in as many different musical techniques as possible. He was interested in Reger, whose complex and overloaded polyphonic style seemd to point towards a composer of an extraordinary virtuosity. Szymanowski was impressed by Reger. The young composer now proceeded along a creative path which was not entirely suited to his own individual talent.

The first works conceived in this new musical atmosphere were a complete fiasco. In a letter to Anna Klechniowska which heralded the first symphony (in E flat major, op. 15)—consisting of two movements only, both composed between 1906 and 1907—Szymanowski wrote, "It is going to be a contrapuntal-harmonic orchestral monster, and I can't wait to see the Berlin critics get up from their seats during the performance of this symphony and sneak out of the hall with a curse on their cyanosed lips."

Fortunately, the composer's predictions turned out to be wrong. This bizarre and false work saw one single performance—as part of a concert given by the Warsaw Philharmonia on March 26th, 1909—and never returned to the concert hall. The next work—a trio for piano, violin, and violoncello—suffered the same fate; in fact, the composer deleted it from the catalogue of his works.

Concurrently with the serious creative crisis came concert failures. In 1907 when the syndicate of young composers re-introduced themselves† to the Warsaw public they were given a cold reception. Although Szymanowski was represented with earlier compositions as well, the works of his colleagues—notably Fitelberg's Symphony—only too clearly showed that they were saturated with German music.

This time Polinski sharply criticized the course the young composers were following. He stated, "They have entered the sphere of some evil spirit who is destroying their creative powers and is determined to rob them of their in-

†After the successful concerts in February 1906.

dividual and national identities and to transform them into parrots ineptly mimicking the voices of Wagner and Richard Strauss." This severe criticism by Polinski caused the members of the syndicate to publish a protest in the press, in which they defended their right to progress.

The crisis in Szymanowski's creative life reached its climax in 1908. Since that fatal concert at the Warsaw Philharmonia, he had sunk into obscurity. While the catalogue of his works had been enriched by new compositions—the "Twelve Songs" op. 17 (setting of poems by various German authors)—no one, alas, could be found who would have been willing to perform these difficult and unrewarding pieces of music. There can be little doubt that the young composer was greatly hurt in his pride and ambition after having been surrounded by the signs of success not so very long before.

At the beginning of this year, Szymanowski travelled to Italy for the first time. He spent February and March at Nervi (near Genoa) on the Mediterranean, where he drafted the song "Penthesilea" (words by Stanislaw Wyspianski from the tragedy *Achilleis*. "I am leading a lazy life, doing nothing and thinking of nothing," he wrote from there to Anna Klechniowska, "and, what is worse, I feel that to a certain extent this indolence is a part of myself." However, in the concluding sentences of the same letter, his discontent and low spirits already gave way to a more optimistic mood. "I shall not be returning to Leipzig† this spring, I shall be going straight home into the country—I need to be alone; I must pull myself together again and work, work endlessly. I have allowed myself to become too demoralized here, too slack. But I do know the harness, and I know how to put it on again."

The Timoshovka ponds.

The composer indeed succeeded in overcoming the crisis and regaining a systematic approach to his creative work. Yet, quite unexpectedly, he turned away from all he had done in the past and started to work on an . . . operetta. With youthful frivolity, he decided to plunge head first from one extreme into another: from what to Polish audiences of that day were unattainable heights of musical sophistication, he threw himself straight into the arms of light music.

Szymanowski hoped to gain success by this means, but overlooked the fact that operetta, being a specific type of music, required a special compositional gift. All the work he had produced so far clearly indicated that his talent lay elsewhere. Undoubtedly, it is no less difficult to produce a good operetta than it is to compose a good symphony, but not everyone who creates good symphonies is a good operettist as well.

On his return from Italy, Szymanowski stayed at Lemberg for a while and from there wrote to Grzegorz Fitelberg, "Under the seal of absolute secrecy, I want to divulge to you that I am returning with two libretti for operettas. But you must, please, not talk about this to anyone. Our fortunes are made." The text for this operetta, which bore three titles (*The Men's Lottery or The Bridegroom No. 69* and *First Prize*), was written for Szymanowski by Julian Krzewinski-Maszynski, son of the well-known composer of choral works Piotr Maszynski. The librettist was a talented comedian and star performer of the operetta ensemble at the Lemberg Theater of that time.

Szymanowski worked on the operetta for the rest of 1908 and throughout the following year. The initial enthusiasm with which he had embarked on the composition of *The Lottery* soon diminished, however. In letters he wrote to Fitelberg in 1909, we keep coming across remarks which clearly indicate that the composer had to muster all his determination in order to complete the operetta. From Timoshovka in October 1909 he wrote to Fitelberg, "The operetta is looming over me like a black cloud of fate, but I am resolved to grit my teeth and finish it before I get to Warsaw. There is not much left to do now." Szymanowski did in fact manage to complete the score of *The Lottery*, but there ends the history of this work. The operetta was never performed.

As it turned out, despite his determination, Szymanowski was not capable of

†A. K. was studying music in Leipzig.

composing anything that was out of keeping with the nature of his creative talent. After the hand-written score of the operetta had, through the mediation of Julian Krzewinski, reached Piotr Maszynski, this experienced composer expressed the following opinion in a letter to his son: "What a pity that this extremely interesting compositional experiment was applied to an object of such insignificance (because that, among all the different forms of music, is what an operetta is). For, the entire score of *First Prize* teems with new effects, some of which are worthy of the most serious music."

The gradual flagging of interest in the operetta as the year 1909 went on was due mainly to the fact that once Szymanowski had completely abandoned the childish plans of wanting to be successful at any price, he immediately got down to such works as would restore his faith in his own abilities. These were the Symphony no. 2 in B flat major, op. 19, and the Piano Sonata no. 2, op. 21. *

Szymanowski eventually succeeded in finding his path in the thicket of German music, and, from the chaos of the varied elements of this music, in creating, as it were, a synthesis of his own. Szymanowski's life now entered one of the most prolific periods. The two years of work spent mainly on the Symphony no. 2 also resulted in several shorter compositions. In addition to the Piano Sonata no. 2, the composer also produced a Romance for Violin and Piano and numerous songs.

In August 1909, he confided to his friend Stefan Spiess, "I feel as if certain little boxes of musical values had newly opened themselves to me . . . In fact, when composing, I enjoy a sense of freedom I have not felt for a very long time."

A year later, a letter to Spiess reveals the following: "Despite the resolution not to do any composing after 4 p.m. but to devote the evenings to reading and making notes, I invariably find myself exceeding the allotted time. My interest in and enthusiasm for the symphony I am working on are simply too great (. . .) This composition is becoming easier and more interesting all the time."

The Symphony in B flat major constituted the climax of Szymanowski's second creative period. Although the later orchestral works by Szymanowski surpass it in value, it has nonetheless retained forever the honor of being the most important symphony in the Polish music of that time. Even if we disregard the profusion of fresh musical ideas contained in this symphony, the high standard of the compositional technique alone in which Szymanowski excelled in this work pushed him irrevocably to the top among Polish composers.

During these years, he also achieved some success in competitions. In 1909, the Berlin musical journal *Signale für die Musikalische Welt* offered prizes for piano pieces. Szymanowski selected one of the fugues in four voices which he had written while still a student at Z. Noskowski's, composed an introduction to it and submitted the whole thing to the journal under the title of "Prelude and Fugue." As a result he received one of the five prizes.

Undoubtedly a more important success, if measurable only against national standards, was the award of first prize for his Piano Sonata no. 1 (op. 8) in a composition competition in 1910. This competition had been arranged by the Lemberg Committee as part of the festivities on the centenary of F. Chopin's birthday.

Szymanowski owed these prizes largely to his earlier compositions. Yet it was not to be very long before his name would once again be associated with important new works in the European world of music.

The first performance of the Symphony no. 2 took place on April 7th, 1911, under Grzegorz Fitelberg. The Warsaw critics reacted rather strangely to Szymanowski's new work. Alexander Polinski, among the first at one time who had not hesitated to refer to the composer as a "genius," altogether failed to understand the new musical language of this symphony. He viciously attacked Szymanowski, by accusing him of having betrayed the musical ideals which the composer had professed in the past. The other critics did not comprehend this work either, but preferred to express their judgment more guardedly – "a little

Szymanowski and his sister in the family's Timoshovka garden

praise, a little reproof" was the approach they chose.

Already when Szymanowski was still working on the Second Symphony and the Second Sonata, a plan was formulated to organize a whole series of concerts with Szymanowski's works in Germany. The performance of the Symphony was, of course, to be held under the leadership of Fitelberg, who, up to the composer's death, consistently launched all his symphonic works on their maiden voyage. Arthur Rubinstein agreed to perform the Sonata. The concerts were eventually given at the turn of the year 1911/1912, but only in Berlin, Leipzig, and Vienna and—as was frequently the case later on—were received more sympathetically abroad than at home.*

It was on the particular occasion of Arthur Rubinstein's performance of the Sonata no. 2 in Cracow in 1912 that Feliks Mangha-Jasienski, in the periodical *Glos Narodu*, wrote the following malicious, yet nonetheless truly prophetic, words: "Masses—undoubtedly—wanted to get to know Szymanowski's new work . . . We must promote our native arts. But . . . does this gentleman already lie buried on the Skalka?† Not yet? Then we will have to wait and see. Once he is buried, we shall make an unprecedentedly enthusiastic din; that is the system we like to adopt. It is always safer not to anticipate the future. Perhaps a great talent, perhaps . . . a great nothing. Who knows? Therefore: Once he lies buried on the Skalka, there is no longer any danger of anyone's making a fool of himself."

The exacting compositional demands Szymanowski had made on himself in these two works were perhaps appreciated most fully by the Viennese critic Richard Specht. "In both works," he wrote, "we find the expression of an absolutely astonishing, original, extremely powerful (and therefore moving) talent—immensely rich in ideas—which although fertilized by the widest variety of musical cultures nevertheless goes its own way . . . Once more we have amongst us someone who feels within himself an urge for great things . . ., someone who does not feel good unless he is able to be creative on a monumental scale."

And all the critics reviewing these concerts agreed with the opinion that, in both his works, the young Polish composer had demonstrated an admirable compositional technique and musical knowledge. If, therefore, Szymanowski once called the Second Symphony a work "such as no Pole had yet composed," then that was no exaggeration. Indeed, it was only thanks to his Symphony and his Sonata that he succeeded in moving to the forefront of European composers of that time, becoming their equal.

Arthur Rubinstein.

The Szymanowski children playing in front of the porch of their Timoshovka home.

*See page 76 for music example 7.

†This is the local name for St. Paul's Church in Cracow (*na Skalce* means "on the little rock"). In the crypts of this church lie the remains of famous Poles. After his death Szymanowski, too, was entombed here.

The Viennese Period

To ensure he did not lose the rank he had managed to attain, Szymanowski decided to leave Warsaw and move to Vienna, as this city was an excellent observation post with respect to the changes that were taking place in European music. A similar decision, also at this time, was made by Szymanowski's friend Grzegorz Fitelberg, despite a certain amount of success the latter had achieved as a conductor at the Warsaw Philharmonia. In the musical circles of Warsaw, the two friends—and Szymanowski in particular—were surrounded by an atmosphere of petty intrigues and by a lack of comprehension. "I am of the opinion," wrote Szymanowski to Fitelberg, "that, despite possible external successes, the two of us—you as well as I—would perpetually be up against all sorts of villainous unpleasantnesses (. . .) That is why I feel it essential, at least for the time being, that we exile ourselves with the greatest urgency."

Since the patron of the publishing syndicate, Prince Wladyslaw Lubomirski, was a popular figure in Viennese society and of far-reaching influence at the court, he was able to provide an artistically easier start for his protégés in what was, after Berlin, the second musical capital of Europe at that time. From then on, Szymanowski spent the major part of the concert season in Vienna, while dedicating the summer and fall to Timoshovka, where he did his most intensive creative work.

The years immediately preceding World War I, which cover the—what we can call—Viennese Period in Szymanowski's life, in many respects played a decisive part in his subsequent musical career. One of the more important events was his coming into contact with the Wiener Universal Edition. This publishing company, whose sphere of activity was worldwide, committed itself to publishing all of Szymanowski's existing and future compositions.

Szymanowski's signature on the contract with Universal Edition marked the final dissolution of the Publishing Syndicate of Young Polish Composers which had once been organized with so great a commitment of forces. This publishing association, so important in the life of the group "Young Poland in Music," had already lost its purpose. The founder of the association, Grzegorz Fitelberg, had virtually stopped composing and opted for a career in conducting. Apolinary Szeluto had been the first to leave the association, after finding it increasingly impossible to keep abreast with his more gifted colleagues. And Ludomir Rozycki had found his publishers in Germany. The contract with Universal Edition brought significant advantages for the young Szymanowski. His works had suddenly gained access to the whole wide world.

During the period in Vienna, Szymanowski experienced the most exuberant years of his youth. The inseparable artistic pair—Szymanowski and Fitelberg—quickly succeeded in attracting the attention of the social elite of Vienna. Both indulged in a splendid mode of life, frequented the best houses, amused themselves in the most expensive taverns, and impressed the snobs of Vienna with their studied elegance. "We have seen for ourselves," Szymanowski wrote to Stefan Spiess, "that the people in Vienna are not that much harder to impress

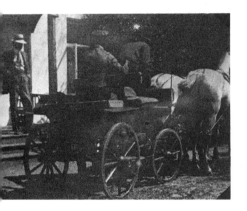

Promenades in horse-drawn coaches were one of the Szymanowskis' favorite pastimes.

than those in Warsaw. If the two of us had more of the nature of comedians and charlatans, we could boast even better results."

Such a flying start in Vienna's artistic and social world would, of course, have been out of the question for either of the two friends had it not been for the considerable help from the always generous Prince Lubomirski who did not deny his gifted protégés anything. Thanks to his recommendation, Szymanowski secured very favorable conditions in his contract with Universal Edition, and thanks to his patronage Fitelberg was given a conductor's post at the Kaiserliche Oper without needing to make the long, arduous climb up the ladder as other *Kappellmeisters* had to do before they could obtain this very high-ranking position in the musical world of Vienna.

Szymanowski's external life at this stage gave the impression of frivolous time-wasting amidst entertainment and amusements, yet simultaneously some very important changes were taking place in his inner life. Up to now, his greatest and most longed-for goal had been the mastery of the compositional craft to the same high standard as that maintained by the most prominent representatives of European music of that time. He had reached this goal in a high degree in the Symphony no. 2 and the Sonata no. 2. Even very severe and exacting critics acknowledged the high technical skill with which the young composer handled the musical material.

Karol Szymanowski, his sister Stanislawa, his father Stanislaw and Gustav Neuhaus in the drawing-room of the Timoshovka home.

The exclusive interest in music had, however, produced certain gaps in the composer's general education, and he now focused his attention on these. "I am really quite uneducated and without preparation," he confessed in a letter to Stefan Spiess. "What is more, I am lazy when it comes to doing any work whatsoever which is not immediately connected with composing." It was necessary, therefore, to make up for what he had missed.

Szymanowski began by reading extensively, mainly philosophical and historical works. Some of the books he read were very popular at that time: *The Birth of Tragedy* by Nietzsche and *Renaissance Culture in Italy* by Jakob Burckhardt. The composer had grown to realize that without a wider intellectual cultivation it is impossible to reach the soaring heights in any of the arts. The conditions in which the fine arts evolve nowadays demand much more than even the most outstanding independent creative gift. A great artist always springs from the matrix of the culture of his time. And since our contemporary culture has been enriched over the centuries by very numerous and varied elements, a universal intellectual gift coupled with great exertion is required in order to absorb this culture as thoroughly as possible and process it mentally for the artist's own use.

Two journeys to Italy, made in the spring of 1910 and 1911 respectively, played a significant part in the inner changes Szymanowski was experiencing. The artistic climate of the old Italian cities, the wandering through the countless art collections and museums, began to exert a strong influence on the crystallization of his artistic ideology. His personal acquaintance with the masterpieces of Italian art, the beauty of which had stood the test of centuries, consolidated in him the belief in the immortality of genuine and uncompromising art.

Under the spell of one of these journeys, he wrote to Zdzislaw Jachimecki: "If only people would see that there is no such thing as original art, that every artist is an aristocrat who must have twelve generations of men like—if he is a musician—Bach and Beethoven and—if he is a poet and dramatist—Sophocles and Shakespeare behind him, and if he. . .renounces his ancestors or does not know them, he will at best be nothing more than a foolish bungler, however great his own individual talent may be. . .If Italy did not exist I, too, could not exist. I am neither a painter nor a sculptor, but when I walk through the rooms of museums, through churches, and finally through the streets, when I look at the noble, proud works of art which smile at everything that is stupid, low, and brainless with their eternally forbearing and serene smile, when I render tangible to the

Above: Karol Szymanowski in 1912. *Below:* Grzegorz Fitelberg, Karol Szymanowski and Arthur Rubinstein in Vienna in 1912.

The manuscript of Szymanowski's
Second Symphony.

senses these whole generations of the most beautiful, most highly gifted human beings, then I feel that it is worthwhile to be alive and to work . . ."

From now on – for many years to come – Italy became the composer's spiritual home. He longed for that country throughout the period of the Great War when, in Timoshovka, the front-line had cut him off from the rest of Europe.

It was during the Viennese period that Szymanowski first began to have doubts about the exclusive excellence of German musical culture. In Vienna he had ample opportunity to get to know contemporary music by composers from a variety of countries. At that time he heard the great opera *Pelléas et Mélisande* by Claude Debussy, but was as yet unable to appreciate its marvelous novelty. He was too much under the spell of Wagner to understand a work which actually constituted a protest against the artistic tyranny of the "Magician from Bayreuth."

On the other hand, the performances by the famous Russian Dyaghilev Ballet in 1913 were watched by him with great interest. Szymanowski was fascinated in particular by the ballet *Petrushka*, a work by his exact contemporary, the young Russian composer Igor Stravinsky. A few months later, after having played through this work on the piano with Arthur Rubinstein and in this way having got to know it very well, he wrote a letter to Stefan Spiess, one sentence of which showed that a turning-point had been reached: "Stravinsky (he of the Russian ballets) is a genius. I am terribly moved by him and consequently have begun to hate the Germans."

During this time, Szymanowski also became interested in exotic themes. At the Kaiserliche Hofbibliothek (Royal Library), on one occasion, he came across poems by Mohammed Hafiz in German translation by Hans Bethge. These white-hot love poems by the greatest Persian lyrical poet from the 14th century enraptured Szymanowski. In the letters he wrote while engaged in setting *The Love Songs of Hafiz* to music, we find several remarks which testify to the powerful creative impulse these poems had released in him. "I am extremely moved by my Hafiz. Allah Himself has thrust him into my hands. I think these texts are ideal," he imparted to Jachimecki.

"I have composed a new song cycle after words by Hafiz, a wonderful poet," we read in a letter to Stefan Spiess. "You cannot imagine what satisfaction this work has been giving me." Eventually, Szymanowski composed two cycles of Hafiz songs. The first cycle – comprising six love poems – was written in 1911 and the second cycle, which consisted of five songs, was composed during the first months of war in 1914.

Between composing one cycle of "Hafiz love songs" and the next, Szymanowski worked on his first opera, *Hagith*. This work, like once the operetta *Men's Lottery,* was intended to "make the composer's career" and "boost his income," as he assured his friends. Since Fitelberg held the conductor's post at the Kaiserliche Oper, it seemed a simple enough matter to Szymanowski to have his opera performed on the stage of this leading opera-house.

However, the hope of producing a work of popular appeal was once again disappointed. Szymanowski chose a one-act libretto by Felix Dörmann which dealt with a somewhat delicate subject from the Bible. Both in the choice of subject and the musical style, the composer used the – at that time very popular – opera *Salomé* by Richard Strauss (libretto by Oscar Wilde) as his model. All efforts to get *Hagith* into the repertoire of the Viennese Opera House failed, however, and when the work was performed in Düsseldorf and Warsaw after the war, it did not arouse a great deal of interest.

Zofia Szymanowska and her brother-in-law Stephen riding on horseback in Timoshovka.

The *Ballets Russes* (Russian
Ballets) company; Diaghilev, the
famous manager, and the cast of
Stravinsky's *Petruschka* which so
impressed Szymanowski.

28

The War Years

In March 1914, Szymanowski travelled to Italy, reached North Africa via Sicily, visited Algiers, Constantine, and Tunis, and then penetrated deeply into the African continent as far as Biskra on the edge of the Sahara. Subsequent stages of this journey led him via Rome and Paris to London. By the time he arrived in the British capital, the nervous disquiet in Europe over the impending catastrophe of war had reached its climax.

Then, when Austria issued its historic ultimatum to Serbia, Szymanowski decided to return to Timoshovka by the shortest possible route. "I got back to my home by the last normal train," he wrote to Spiess. "We are all in a state of panic and shock. I ought to get down to work really—wanted to compose a piano concerto—but under the circumstances I do not know whether it will be possible."

Gradually, however, the panic subsides. And what is more curious still: quite unexpectedly the composer feels a desire to join the army. "I sometimes regret," he writes to a friend, "that my leg does not permit me to go to war. Have you noticed that at times like these every man suddenly has something of an old adventurer awakening inside him—even quiet individuals such as I?"

In Timoshovka, which was still a long way from the front-line, life soon returned to normal. The only indication of there being a war on was the wounded soldiers and the convalescents accommodated on the estate.

Szymanowski now reflected deeply on the rich impressions he had gained on the last journey. These travels were to have a decisive influence on the shaping of his artistic attitudes over the next few years. Above all, he decided to make a complete break with German music and "go over" to the Romance musical culture. Later, this resolution was to result in a change of direction for the development of the whole of Polish music.

Mediator in this radical change was Igor Stravinsky whose ballet *Petrushka* had once, in Vienna, aroused Szymanowski's interest. In London he had got to know Stravinsky personally and heard his new works, which finally convinced him that the further development of European music would certainly not proceed along the lines of a more or less successful Wagner imitation, but would take nourishment from the works of French impressionists: Debussy and Ravel.

Another thing the journey did was to revive Szymanowski's earlier interest in Arabic culture, with which he had come into close contact in North Africa. He now obtained extensive scientific literature in order to improve his knowledge of Arabic history and culture. No less strong were the impressions his stay in Sicily had made on him—where the strange history of this island was reflected in numerous architectural monuments bearing witness to the frequent changes of rulership that took place over the centuries: from Greeks to Romans to Arabs and Vikings. His interest extended further to Hellenic culture and thence to the early history of Christianity. Szymanowski ended up with a wide circle of historical and philosophical problems, the assimilation of which kept him occupied all through the war.

These interesting historical and philosophical studies brought the composer

Igor Stravinsky.

closer to literature. It was during this time that he discovered his literary talent and began to explore his capabilities in this field. From then on, literature occupied an important position in his life, or did rather more than that: it pervaded his musical creations. Theretofore, Szymanowski's instrumental music had been influenced neither by literature nor by painting, but had been based on the concept of absolutely free music. Now, swayed by his interest in new artistic fields, he began to turn to programme music and strove to express literary contents by musical means.

His compositions from the first year of war bear the marks of a transitional stage. When the first shock caused by the outbreak of war had worn off and conditions had returned to normal, Szymanowski did not start work on the piano concerto he had planned to compose, but returned to *The Love Songs of Hafiz*, adding a new cycle of five songs to that produced before the war. The broadly structured piano part of the first cycle, which, with its rich chromaticism, sought to emulate the sultry atmosphere of the Hafiz poems, did not yet satisfy the composer. *

Zofia Szymanowska.

When composing the second cycle, he transferred the accompaniment to orchestra. Only the rich scale of the instrumental timbre made it possible for him to recreate Hafiz' passionate hymns in praise of love and wine congenially in music. At that time, he also arranged three songs from the first cycle for orchestra. After the World War, the two cycles were performed as a ballet at the Warsaw Opera House.

September 1914 saw the birth of a plan to create a longer work in the new style. In the fall and winter, the composer drafted part of his Third Symphony, which was to incorporate a solo part for a tenor and a choir. The text on which this "symphonic cantata" is based once again derives from Persian poetry. This time the composer chose "The Song of the Night" by the medieval Persian mystic Jebad ad-Din Rumi. Work on the symphony was interrupted by a journey to Kiev during the winter season. The composer did not complete the symphony until 1916, and dispensed with the separate finale he had originally thought of, instead adding a brief ending to what he had composed earlier. **

After the second cycle of *The Love Songs of Hafiz*, the Symphony no. 3, consisting of a single movement, marks the next step on the road towards the attainment of a new style. Here, too, the tone-colors produced by the orchestra create a mood of the greatest emotional intensity, which pervades the whole of this "symphonic cantata." This is one of the composer's most ecstatic works.

In Kiev Szymanowski had come across his friend, the outstanding violinist Pawel Kochanski, a meeting which gave his compositional interests a completely new direction. He now began to work on a cycle of violin pieces which he called *Myths*. In this cycle, Szymanowski achieved his new instrumental style with a clear tendency towards programme music. All pieces of the cycle spring from the composer's interest in the world of antiquity.

The origin of the first piece – "The Source of the Arethusa" – goes back to the composer's memories of Sicily. In the port of Syracuse, on the small island of Ortygia, there is a spring which, according to legend, is linked beneath earth and ocean with the river Alphios in Arcadia. Both this source and the river have been named after the heroes of the legend: the nymph Arethusa and the god Alphios who, in love with Arethusa, pursues her through the tunnel under the sea to as far as the island of Ortygia. The second piece – "Narcissus" – is based on the legend of the beautiful Narcissus who has fallen in love with his reflection in the water. The third piece – "Dryads and Pan" – illustrates a popular mythological scene: the wooing of the wood nymphs by the god Pan.

Almost parallel with *Myths*, Szymanowski composed a piano cycle which was given the title *Metopes*. The Greek metopes (bas-reliefs with scenes from mythology) he had recently seen at the museum in Palermo had given him the idea to set to music three themes from Homer's *Odyssey*. The three *Metopes* by Szymanowski were entitled "Island of the Sirens," "Calypso," and "Nausicaa."

*See page 77 for music example 8; **see page 77 for music examples 9 and 10.

The manuscript of *The Love Songs of Hafiz*, Szymanowski's vocal instrumental cycle.

Above: **The tennis court in Timoshovka.** *Below:* **Karol Szymanowski and Pawel Kochanski in 1916 in Zaruzdie, where Szymanowski worked on his Violin Concerto No. 1 and Kochanski advised him on the solo part.**

In spite of deriving from the same creative base, *Metopes* and *Myths* differ considerably in their artistic value. The *Metopes* composed for piano are overloaded with sound, because the color effects intended by the composer are lost in the dense mass of sound. The keyboard, in this composition, is almost ceaselessly being worked to the utmost limit of the pianistically possible.

In his *Myths*, on the other hand, Szymanowski was able to elicit the most exquisite timbre from the violin and to create that peculiar impressionist style of his own. There is no doubt that the *Myths* are equal in their artistic quality to the impressionist piano style of Debussy and Ravel. It is largely to these three pieces for violin that Szymanowski owes his popularity in European music. Nowadays there is unlikely to be any violinist of any standing anywhere in the world who does not include *Myths* in his repertoire. *

In 1915, Szymanowski made another attempt to work out an impressionist style for the piano. He produced a new cycle of three piano pieces with the collective title *Masks*. While the previous cycles consisted of programme music, the matter becomes more complicated where the *Masks* are concerned. The headings of the three *Masks*—"Sheherazade," "Tantris the Fool," and "Don Juan's Serenade"—do not signify a continuous narrative. Szymanowski's intention was to make a parody of the three characters chosen here, and he conveyed this purpose in the apt title of *Masks*.

In a letter to Stefan Spiess dating from the time the *Masks* were being composed, we read, "I have just completely finished my 'Don Juan' and feel extremely happy about it! Despite a certain parodic style—no, because of it—it is worth more than those Odyssey compositions" (which, of course, refers to the *Metopes*).

The parody intended in the *Masks* relies purely on literary assumptions, however. Here Szymanowski the musician and Szymanowski the literary man have probably come closer together than anywhere else. Unfortunately, the person listening to the *Masks* will fail to recognize what is being assumed, since it is literary characters that are being parodied and not popular musical motives. In addition to the characters that are generally known—Sheherazade and Don Juan—, Szymanowski also includes a certain Tantris among his *Masks*. This is in fact Tristan, the famous hero of the well-known drama of chivalry. Under this anagrammatized name and disguised as a fool, Tristan arrives at the court of King Mark to see his beloved Isolde once more.

Again, in *Masks*, the composer has failed to avoid an overloading with sound. The reproduction of such an impressive abundance of musical ideas as is found in this work almost goes beyond the range of the piano's possibilities—it seems as though we were confronted with an orchestra restricted to the limits of the piano. Szymanowski was well aware of this shortcoming of *Masks*, and, during the last few years of his life, intended to re-write this work for piano with orchestral accompaniment. Unfortunately, however, he was not to complete this task. **

Immediately after finishing *Masks*, Szymanowski began with the composition of the First Violin Concerto, op. 35. The month of August 1916 he spent at Zarudzie, an estate belonging to his friend Jozef Jaroszynski, where Pawel Kochanski was also staying at that time. Within a few weeks, the composer had drafted the whole concerto, enlisting Kochanski's help when constructing the solo parts for the violin. "I must say I am very pleased with the whole thing," he wrote to Spiess from Zarudzie. "Once again there are some new little notes while a bit of the old style has been reverted to at the same time. The work as a whole is terribly fanciful and unexpected."

In the creative life of Szymanowski, the Violin Concerto no. 1 signified the gradual return to absolute music. Strictly speaking, the work consists of a single movement only. It can, however, be readily differentiated into four separate parts corresponding to the traditional symphonic form. Only the first two movements, which take the place of the classical allegro and the andante, are of the nature of programme music.

Alexander Scriabin

As proved by Zdzislaw Jachimecki in his work on Szymanowski,† the composer used the poem "Night in May" (from the cycle *By Star-light at Dusk*) by Tadeusz Micinski as a poetic programme. The scherzo and finale, on the other hand, represent an entirely independent further development of the concerto. The poem by Micinski thus had the function of a propelling force which stimulated Szymanowski's imagination and enabled him to reproduce a certain emotional atmosphere, for it was not the composer's intention to transcribe Micinski's poem into musical language. The Violin Concerto no. 1 is again an ecstatic work of special allure which readily gained recognition by the whole of the musical world. *

In connection with the First Violin Concerto, it is appropriate to go into the nature of Kochanski's collaboration in Szymanowski's works for violin. It is but little known that Szymanowski was familiar with the violin from practical experience. He had played the violin in his youth, particularly during his stay in Lemberg in 1907. Pawel Kochanski, who was among the most prominent violinists of that time, demonstrated to the composer above all the latest achievements of his violin technique and in addition—as can be seen from the drafts that still exist—edited the violin part as regards fingering and bowing. Occasionally, where the violin parts were particularly uncomfortable, he also suggested amendments or advised a more effective solution. The only exclusive accomplishment on Kochanski's part as far as the Violin Concerto no. 1 is concerned, is the solo cadenza of the violin towards the end of the concerto.

Despite the war, the composer's way of life did not (until 1917) differ a great deal from what it used to be in peace-time. He spent the winter season in Kiev—where all the wealthier landowners from the Ukraine went at this time of the year—to partake of the pleasures of social life. For the summer, the Szymanowski family returned to Timoshovka. Here, the composer locked himself into the wooden garden pavilion—known among the family as "kompozytornia" (something like "composing studio")—for hours on end, and worked.

What grieved him most of all at that time was the impossibility of travelling abroad. He had hoped to do so in order to introduce, as quickly as possible, his new works, which differed so significantly from all his pre-war compositions. However, this problem too did not remain unresolved.

Until recently, Szymanowski had had virtually no contact with musical centers in Russia. Now, in wartime, he made several journeys to Russia in which he managed to open relations with composers, soloists, and publishers. He owed a lot, in this respect, to Mrs. Natalia Dawydow, a rich landowner and neighbor and an ardent admirer of his talent, who, thanks to her numerous social contacts, paved the way into the Russian musical world for him.

Pawel Kochanski, who was staying in Petersburg at that time, zealously publicized his friend's compositions. By the end of 1916, the ground had been sufficiently prepared. In the next concert season in Petersburg, three premieres of Szymanowski's works were to take place: Pawel Kochanski was to play the Violin Concerto no. 1, which had just been completed, the pianist Sasza Dubjanski prepared the performance of *Masks*, and for January 1917 the first performance of the Symphony no. 3 under Siloti was announced.

During that time, the negotiations with the big publishing company Jurgenson from Moscow that had been going on for several months were also approaching their favorable conclusion. The composer was, therefore, close to realizing his hopes of having his latest compositions published. There is no doubt that the always abundant and varied musical life in Russia made up to a high degree for Szymanowski's lack of contact with other countries.

Reading Szymanowski's correspondence from that time, it would appear as if all the concerns of his musical life which occupied him so much in those days were

---

†Z. Jachimecki: *Karol Szymanowski. Rys dotychczasowej tworczosci* (Outline of his work so far), Cracow (1927).

*See pages 80-81 for music example 13.

happening in some country where no one had ever heard about war. The composer does not even seem to have had any premonition of the events which were soon to shatter all his plans. Consequently, when the first revolutionary tremors made themselves felt in Russia, they took him completely by surprise. He did not comprehend the changes that were taking place around him. All he could see was that the world in which he grew up and had been living, suddenly went to rack and ruin. All this appeared like a nightmare to him. Weakened by a severe attack of scarlet fever which he had suffered in the early months of 1917 and numbed by the rapid course of political events, he sank into a state of total apathy.

It was not until the summer of this year – and it was his last summer in Timoshovka – that he started to compose again. He simply ran away from a reality that was incomprehensible to him and sought refuge in the abstract sphere of art. This summer resulted in the production of the Piano Sonata no. 3, the String Quartet no. 1, and two cantatas, *Agave* and *Demetrio* on texts by Zofia Szymanowski.

In the course of this intense creativity he regained calm of mind: "What luck that my nerves are much better than in the spring," he related to Spiess. "I must tell you, I have gone through a rather interesting evolution in respect of what is happening around me. I have come fully to terms with myself, which explains my comparatively good humor and a certain amount of inner peace."

In the two most important works of this period, i.e., the Sonata no. 3 and the String Quartet no. 1, Szymanowski finally returned to absolute music. Although the Sonata makes use of the same impressionist means in its musical material as those we encounter in the earlier piano cycles (*Metopes, Masks*), their purpose here is a different, new, one. There, they were intended to express certain literary contents; here, they become the artistic purpose *per se*. The Sonata is one of the most abstract piano works by Szymanowski and at the same time the most difficult of all his compositions for this instrument. Although – like the first Violin Concerto – it actually consists of a single movement only, it can be broken down into four movements in keeping with the traditional sonata: an allegro, a slow movement, a scherzo, and a finale. As in the earlier sonatas, here too the finale takes the form of a fugue. This fugue is one of the highest manifestations of Szymanowski's talent in the domain of polyphony. *

Significantly, Szymanowski's turning-away from programme music – and the Piano Sonata no. 3 is the first complete realization of this renunciation – occurred simultaneously with the start of his work on the great novel *Ephebos*. The first notes and drafts for this novel date from precisely that period. Thus, his creative endeavors now flowed in two separate streams: a musical and a literary one.

The First String Quartet, composed immediately after the Sonata no. 3, is remarkable particularly on account of its sound atmosphere. The composer who in the Sonata made consistent use of dissonance, now softens his sound effects. In this respect, the last movement of the Quartet – "the Burlesque" – is especially interesting, since a classical polytonal technique has been used in its construction. Every voice has a different key assigned to it, yet the result of this is not the cacophony one might expect, but a sound effect of surprising harmony.

The Quartet in three movements by Szymanowski is in reality an unfinished work. Originally it was meant to consist of four movements. What is now the concluding "Burlesque" was intended as a scherzo, whereas the finale was to take the form of a fugue. After composing three movements of the Quartet in the summer of 1917, Szymanowski could not muster the necessary energy to complete the work. In 1922, he submitted it to the Ministry for the People's Education as his entry to a competition and was awarded the first prize for it. The only alteration he made when preparing the work for publication was to change the sequence of the movements. The String Quartet no. 1 now belongs to the most readily comprehensible of the works Szymanowski wrote during the war.

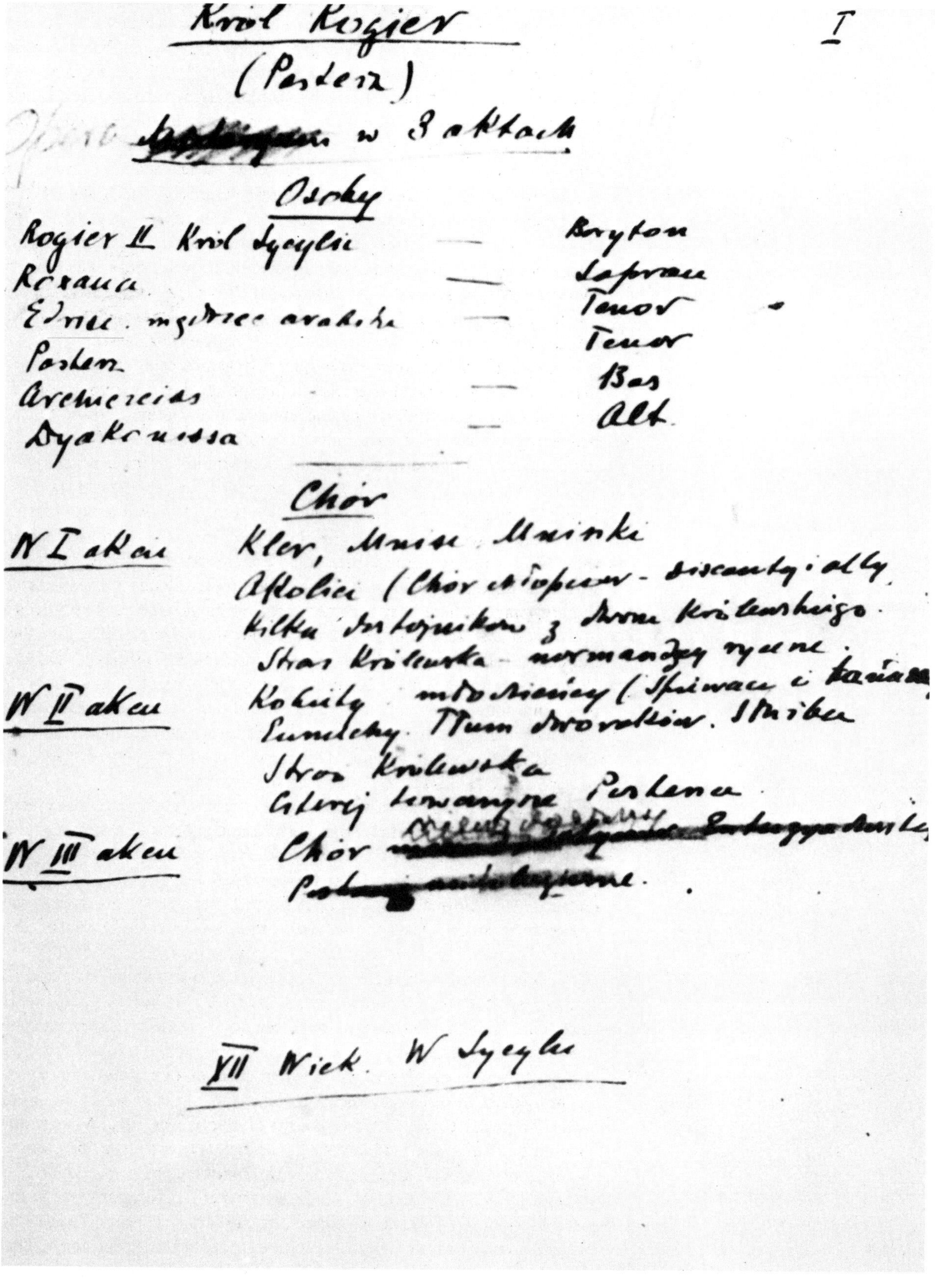

Król Rogier

(Pasterz)

~~Opera~~ w 3 aktach

Osoby

Rogier II. Król Sycylii — Bryton
Roxana — Sopran
Edris. mędrzec arabski — Tenor
Pasterz — Tenor
Arcimereias — Bas
Dyakonissa — Alt

Chór

W I akcie   Kler, Mnisi Mniszki
Akolici (Chór chłopców - discanty i alty
kilku dostojników z dworu królewskiego.
Straż królewska - normandzy rycerze

W II akcie   Kobiety młodzieńcy (śpiewacy i tancerze
Eunuchy. Tłum dworaków. Straże

Straż królewska
Czterej towarzysze Pasterza

W III akcie   Chór ~~...~~
Pasterze ~~...~~

XII Wiek. W Sycylii

The manuscript of the
libretto for the operetta *King
Roger*.

36

Ephebos

Szymanowski in Knights of Malta uniform.

In October 1917, the Szymanowskis were forced to leave Timoshovka forever. They took up residence in Yelisavetgrad, to which they also managed to transport a portion of the old furniture and historical mementos. Not long after the Szymanowskis had departed, their country house in Timoshovka was destroyed by fire.

These events disrupted one of the most intensely creative periods in the composer's life. Whereas he had worked very hard in Timoshovka as if gripped by a feverish excitement, he now gave up composing altogether and lost himself in futile speculation. Numerous problems which had been accumulating inside him since the beginning of the war – caused not only by his memories of the journey to Sicily and Africa and his extensive reading but also by the events of the revolution that was raging round him – were pressing to be released.

Szymanowski began to write. In the course of the next two years evolved the draft of a novel called *Ephebos*†. In these pages, the author resolves the moral and philosophical questions which have been worrying him for so long. Sealed off by the walls of his study from the ugly small town where, as he writes, "one's eye and good taste are mortally offended by every lane and every house," Szymanowski evokes memories of the Italian landscape which forms the background to the plot of his novel.

Ephebos did not just make Szymanowski's problems less painful for him. The literary activity to which by now he had become passionately attached also represented an escape from reality into the past. The fatalistic mood into which he had sunk as a result of contemporary events, finds its expression in the many notes written on the sheets of the draft. There we find the following confession: "The writing of books often turns into a burial of the writer's own dreams of life, into a farewell for all eternity, into lonely weeping over a fresh grave."

In conjunction with *Ephebos*, in which the painful questions of his philosophy of life were expressed in literary form, Szymanowski tried to unravel certain problems in a purely theoretical way. Evidence of this is the fragments of short philosophical treatises that have been preserved among his papers.

The war continued, and in June 1918 Yelisavetgrad was occupied by Austrian and German troops. The composer grasped an opportunity to enter into correspondence with his publishers from Vienna, the Universal Edition. This served to revive his interest in musical affairs. Szymanowski started to go through and correct all the works he had composed during the war. They needed to be prepared for the printer. The director of Universal Edition, Emil Hertzka, pleaded with the composer to come to Vienna. The temptation was strong, but consideration for his family – who would have had to be left to an uncertain fate in Yelisavetgrad – made him decide against the project.

It was at this time, too, that he conceived the idea of composing an opera with a theme relating to his Sicilian memories. Szymanowski invited his cousin Jaroslaw Iwaszkiewicz, who was then taking his first steps into the field of literature, to help with the libretto. The composer did not yet have faith in his

†An ephebe, in ancient Greece, was a young man old enough to go to war. The novel by Karol Szymanowski was destroyed by fire in Warsaw in 1939 and no longer exists. Recently (in 1981) a chapter from *Ephebos*—in a Russian translation by the author himself—was found in Paris.

own literary ability and preferred to draw on the poet's assistance for producing a libretto in verse. In the summer of 1918, Iwaszkiewicz visited the composer in Yelisavetgrad and it was there, during their long discussions, that the first outlines of the action of *King Roger* (at that stage still referred to simply as the "Sicilian tragedy") began to emerge.

After leaving Yelisavetgrad, Iwaszkiewicz made a rough draft of the libretto, and afterwards met with the composer again in Odessa, where they continued to discuss the drama in detail. During these discussions, Szymanowski sought to convey all his Sicilian and African impressions to Iwaszkiewicz, even telling him about the contents of the books he had read. In short, he wanted to acquaint his cousin with the intellectual atmosphere in which he lived. The young poet absorbed every word. The longing for the beauty of the Sicilian landscape began to grab hold of him, too, and he was full of enthusiasm for the exotic magic of Arabic culture.

On his train journey to Odessa, where he was to meet the composer, Iwaszkiewicz drafted six short poems on the pages of his pocket diary. These poems were given the collective title *Songs of the Infatuated Muezzin*. They are, of course, an echo of Szymanowski's recollections of Africa. These poems fired the composer's creative imagination. For the moment his novel was forgotten. Within a few days after his return to Yelisavetgrad, he had set his cousin's poems to music. Szymanowski tried, in these songs, to catch the essence of the oriental atmosphere. The music is full of chromaticisms and embellished coloraturas. The *Songs of the Infatuated Muezzin* belong to those of Szymanowski's works which are "over-adorned in Baroque fashion, smell of musk, and are oppressive, even if also beautiful," as Iwaszkiewicz later so aptly described them.*

The joint work on the libretto for the new opera was interrupted for a considerable time. In October 1918 Iwaszkiewicz managed to make his way to Warsaw, whereas Szymanowski returned to Yelisavetgrad and resumed work on the novel *Ephebos*, while waiting for Iwaskiewicz to send him the libretto from Warsaw. "I feel that my hunger for writing has been satisfied," he wrote to August Iwanski in January 1918, "and that I shall be returning to music with pleasure. Naturally my approach to music will be a different one from now on—I want music that stimulates my poetic instincts as well." Nevertheless, Szymanowski continued to work on the second volume of his *Ephebos* for the rest of the year.

He waited in vain for the libretto. As soon as Iwaszkiewicz had arrived in Warsaw, he opened relations with the Scamander Group, achieved his first successes as a writer, and understandably was unable to revive Szymanowski's Sicilian longings within himself. The composer, however, was in complete ignorance of the new situation Iwaszkiewicz now found himself in. Every so often, therefore, when writing to friends in Warsaw, he enquired after the fate of the libretto.

Felix, Karol and Stanislawa Szymanowski in Elisavetgrad.

*See page 82 for music example 15.

The Return to Poland

Towards the end of 1919, Szymanowski decided to leave Yelisavetgrad for good. By a roundabout route via Rumania, he arrived in Warsaw in December, alone. The rest of the family did not return to Poland until the following February.

His joy over the return to Poland did not last long, however. As it turned out, the unfriendly attitude adopted to his works by the musical public of Warsaw had not modified at all. When, at a concert in the hall of the Warsaw Conservatory, Szymanowski introduced his wartime creations, the audience present was more than sparse. And the critics received his works with unconcealed dislike.

"The concert here," Szymanowski wrote to Zdislaw Jachimecki, "has given me a lot to think about, and I am feeling rather bitter. Once again I was faced with the same realization that seven years ago forced me to leave Warsaw—namely, that between me and the Polish (or at least the Warsaw) public there is no real contact, that I am incomprehensible to this audience and—in view of the general structure of Polish music—perhaps even dispensable, a typical nonentity who serves only to prove what inferior minds the Warsaw musicians generally are. The European atmosphere of my art simply will not go down with these provincials. I am an embarrassment to them, because I expose and unmask them (. . .). Despite the participation of Pawel Kochanski—who has always, and very rightly, had a tremendous success here—and of my sister who, as you well know, is also utterly deserving of such success, the hall was not sold out. In other words, there were not 600 persons in Warsaw who were interested in what I have been doing during the last five years. You must admit that that is no joke. I think of what would happen in Petersburg or in Moscow if a Scriabin or Rachmaninov were to return and give a performance after five years. It is possible that those two are worth more than I, but one has to cut one's coat according to one's cloth—we simply do not have musicians of such greatness here."

While in this frame of mind, Szymanowski gradually formed the resolution to go abroad. Meanwhile, however, he took an active part in the musical life of Warsaw. Under contract with the Central Propaganda Committee, he turned his attention to organizing concerts for soldiers and composing marches. At the same time, however, he persuaded Iwaszkiewicz to finish the libretto for *King Roger*.

While Iwaszkiewicz was writing the final verses of the libretto, Szymanowski composed a short ballet called *Mandragora* for the Polish Theater in Warsaw. This work is a typical *commedia dell'arte*, modelled by the composer on the humoresques the Szymanowski siblings used to arrange in Timoshovka a long time ago. In this instance, *Mandragora* was intended as the conclusion of the comedy *Le Bourgeois Gentilhomme* by Molière in a performance at the Polish Theater. *Mandragora* was endowed with roguish and witty music by its composer. It was performed many times in Warsaw and later also abroad—in the latter case purely as a ballet, not in conjunction with Molière's comedy.

In June 1920, Iwaszkiewicz at last presented the finished libretto for *King Roger*. Szymanowski began his composition with great enthusiasm, but it soon turned out that for him, too, the theme dug up from his Sicilian recollections had lost much of its attraction. Nor is it likely that Szymanowski remained unaffected by the change of environment. What had appeared to glitter in beautiful and alluring colors in his hermitage in Yelisavetgrad now, in contact with the real and colorful life of Warsaw, turned pale and grey. But he did not abandon the work. By October 1920, the draft of the opera had reached the opening bars of the second act. The composition was interrupted by his first journey to America.*

For some time, Szymanowski and his friend Jan Effenberg-Sliwinski had been making preparations for a publicity tour to various European cities on the instructions of what was then the Office for Overseas Propaganda. They intended to organize concerts and exhibitions of Polish art on this tour. While still in the middle of these preparations, Szymanowski came to London, where he met Pawel Kochanski and Arthur Rubinstein. Persuaded by them, he cancelled the arrangement with the Office for Overseas Propaganda and, instead of travelling to Scandinavia as had originally been planned, he went to America.

Rubinstein, who had spent the whole of the war in the West, had precisely at this time moved to the very top among European pianists and was achieving success particularly in America. He now resolved that his friends should have an easier start on the musical rostra of the world. That was the purpose of this journey. However, only Pawel Kochanski got off the ground and quickly occupied an important rank among American virtuosi. Szymanowski, on the other hand, was of course not the type of composer who could have made a career for himself in a flash, American-style. Not only the specific gravity of his compositions made this impossible, but also his aversion to any kind of compromise where art was concerned.

Nevertheless, the stay in America turned out to be useful for him too. He managed to establish numerous contacts in international musical circles and became acquainted with many conductors and virtuosi. This subsequently helped to popularize his works all over the world. His friend's failure did nothing to make Rubinstein feel discouraged, however. In the following concert season, he gave Szymanowski the opportunity to try again, by inviting him to America a second time.

Szymanowski and Kochanski on a ship, on their way to America.

*See page 83 for music example 16.

The Period of National Inspiration

On the return journey from America in May 1921, Szymanowski experienced one of the most important moments in his career as a composer. As seven years earlier, he met up with Igor Stravinsky in London and – as before – the influence the Russian composer had on him, caused fundamental changes in Szymanowski's artistic ideology. Their encounter before the war had persuaded him to break his ties with German music and go over to French musical culture. Now, under the influence of Stravinsky's new works, he decided to affiliate his music with Polish folk-music. This marked the onset of what was to be the most important period in his creative life: the national period.

Already in his earlier ballets, Stravinsky had made abundant use of Russian folklore. He had known how to recast this music so that it enchanted with its original rhythm and its lively colors. One of the compositions that aroused a genuine enthusiasm in Szymanowski was Stravinsky's ballet *Petrushka*. But Stravinsky's style had undergone further development during the war years. His latest composition, the ballet *Les Noces*, on which he was then engaged and from which he played excerpts on the piano for the Polish composer, penetrated with curious artistic intuition into the deepest layers of Russian folk-music. Musical quotations were no longer necessary here. The highly gifted composer knew how to express the nature of "Russian-ness" in an exquisite way by his own artistic means. The impact made by *Les Noces* was tremendous.

At the beginning of 1921, Szymanowski returned to Poland. He intended to spend the whole summer at home and to travel to America again in the fall. On his desk lay the opera *King Roger*, awaiting completion. The composer found it quite impossible to return to the – as he called it – "Sicilian tragedy," however. He had moved too far away from the state of mind which, way back during the war, had given him the idea to write this opera. New artistic impressions had pushed his interests into another direction.

After several weeks at his home, he wrote to Arthur Rubinstein: "Apart from a few little songs, I have written nothing so far. I intend to get down to finishing the opera, but it is difficult. I have let the break get too long, and my interest in it has flagged already."

These "few little songs" are the *Slopiewnie*† based on poems by Julian Tuwim. In these songs, Szymanowski tried to create an ancient Slavonic style. The *Slopiewnie* operate by the joining-together of roots of Polish words from which the poet creates new concepts, comprehensible only through their connotational value. From the composer's point of view, this made them an almost ideal base from which to work out the new style he was striving for. *

Apart from *Slopiewnie*, Szymanowski wrote an enthusiastic essay on Stravinsky that summer in which he referred to him as "the absolutely greatest living composer."

The preference for oriental exoticism Szymanowski had shown during World War I had derived from the need to find some original basis for his creative work which would enrich his music with new elements. We already know that his en-

†The Polish word "slopiewnie" was made up by Tuwim. The English equivalent would be something like "wordsongs" (an equally artificial word-construction).

*See page 83 for music example 17.

thusiasm for exotic cultures appeared suddenly just at that moment when he had become fully aware of the hollowness of post-Wagnerian German music as well as of the danger threatening his own creative work, which until then had been so closely connected with German music.

The two cycles of *The Love Songs of Hafiz*, the Symphony no. 3, the *Songs of the Infatuated Muezzin*—these are major works, which sprang from his admiration for Arabic-Persian culture. No less important an influence on Szymanowski's compositions at that time was the culture of antiquity, as evidenced by *Metopes, Masks,* and the cantatas *Demetrio* and *Agave*. And the opera *King Roger* became the synthesis of these two cultures. By such remote paths, Szymanowski gradually approached the discovery of an exotic musical culture in his own country: Podhale music.†

Bringing himself to draw on Polish folk-music was not easy for Szymanowski, because it meant he had to overcome certain deep-rooted prejudices. Ever since setting himself the lofty goal of reaching a European standard with his works, he looked at the applicability of musical folklore in composition with considerable skepticism. Basically, it seemed frivolous to him and unworthy of a serious composer. This attitude resulted from what was happening in Polish music at that time, where particularly the weaker composers covered up their poverty of melodic invention by using folk-music.

As early as in 1907, he had, in a letter to Zdzislaw Jachimecki, referred to such practices as "dilettantism and reliance on popular national, idyllic Oberek motives."†† If his work was to climb above the average contemporary Polish music, it had to distance itself, at least for the time being, from expressing its Polish character in this way. "No one should look for cosmopolitanism in my music or—worse still—for internationalism," he defended himself against the attacks of the critics. "Only a 'European quality' can be found in it, and that does not constitute a repudiation of the 'Polish quality.' " It was not until after the World War that Szymanowski's attitude to using folk-music as material in a composition was to change.

Szymanowski's first encounter with Gorale music took place several months after his return to Poland. In March 1920, a concert of works by him was given in which his sister Stanislawa and Pawel Kochanski participated. After the concert, the then-director of the Lemberg Conservatory, Adam Soltys, held a reception at his residence in honor of the composer, and it was there that Szymanowski came into contact with Professor Adolf Chybinski, a musicologist. The latter was at that particular time engaged in collecting the musical folklore of the Podhale region—in collaboration with Julius Zborowski, the director of the Tatra Museum.††† Professor Chybinski drew Szymanowski's attention to certain original peculiarities of the Podhale melodies—among them the fact that these melodies have their own special scale and that in some cases their structure indicates the origin of music such as is played on the bagpipes.

Szymanowski betrayed an interest in these matters and listened attentively to the melodies Professor Chybinski played to him on the piano. Soon afterwards it was to turn out that the seed had fallen on fertile ground. One melody in particular appealed to the composer. It appears at the beginning of the song "Holy Francis" from the *Slopiewnie* by Tuwim, and it also forms the opening of Szymanowski's great ballet *Harnasie.*

It seems strange that Szymanowski had not noticed the Gorale music at all during his numerous visits to Zakopane before the World War, for he must have had ample opportunity to listen to it. It was only the enthusiastic attitude of the Lemberg musicologist that enabled him to see its curious beauty, which he now tried to capture in the sound constructions of his art.

When staying in London for a prolonged period before his first trip to America, Szymanowski met Sergei Dyaghilev, the creator of the famous "Ballets russes," which for several years caused a sensation in the art world throughout

---

†"Podhale" the Polish name for the landscape at the foot of the High Tatra around the town of Zakopane. This area is inhabited by the "mountain-dwellers" ("gorale" in Polish). ††*Oberek* is a lively Polish folk dance. †††This museum is in Zakopane.

Igor Strawiński

The manuscript of Szymanowski's article on Igor Stravinsky. "It is very important for us to know his work because of his attitude towards national elements in music."

SALA KONSERWATORJUM

(Ul. Okólnik № 1.)

W Sobotę d. 24 go Stycznia 1920 r. o godz. 7-ej wiecz.

KONCERT KOMPOZYTORSKI

KAROLA SZYMANOWSKIEGO

Udział w koncercie wezmą:

Stanisława SZYMANOWSKA (śpiew)

Paweł KOCHAŃSKI (skrzypce)

Przy fortepianie: Karol SZYMANOWSKI

Feliks SZYMANOWSKI

PROGRAM:

Część I.

1. Parafrazy „Caprices" Paganini'ego
   a) D-dur
   b) A-dur
   c) A-moll (Thema variés)
   (skrzypce i fortepian) wyk. P. Kochański i K. Szymanowski

2. Pieśni
   Z cyklu „Barwne pieśni" op. 22
   a) Przeznaczenie
   b) Do małych dziewczynek
   c) Pieśń dziewczęcia z okna
   Z cyklu „Miłosne pieśni Hafiza" op. 25
   d) Życzenia
   e) Taniec

3. „Mity" op. 30
   a) Zdrój Aretuzy
   b) Narcyz
   c) Dryady i Pan
   odśp. St. Szymanowska akomp. Fel. Szymanowski

Część II.

4. Pieśni
   a) Zuleika (z op. 13)
   Z cyklu „Muza szalony" op. 42
   b) „Allah"
   c) „O, ukochana ma"
   Z cyklu „Pieśni Księżniczki z baśni" op. 36
   d) „Słowik"
   odśp. St. Szymanowska, akomp. Fel. Szymanowski

5. „Notturno e Tarantella" op. 28
   (skrzypce i fortepian) wyk. P. Kochański i K. Szymanowski

„PARNASSION" — Warszawa, Hortensja 6, tel. Dyr. 256,
Sekr. 323 (dawny).

Program of a 1920 Szymanowski recital at the Warsaw Conservatory Hall, with Pawel Kochanski playing the violin, the composer's sister Stanislawa singing the vocal parts, and Karol Szymanowski and his brother Feliks at the piano.

44

the whole of Europe. Already during World War I, Szymanowski had toyed with the idea of composing the music for a ballet. This genre had attained a very high artistic rank at that time, due in no small part to Dyaghilev, who had known how to arouse the interest of the most outstanding European composers.

Szymanowski intended to use his London encounter with Dyaghilev to obtain a commission from him for a ballet. Unfortunately, this plan did not succeed. The Dyaghilev ensemble was just going through a serious crisis which threatened to result in the imminent dissolution of the whole group. No wonder, then, that under these circumstances Dyaghilev was in no hurry to commission new ballets. The "ballet problem" did not cease to occupy Szymanowski, however.

In Warsaw, at the beginning of June 1921, the composer met two friends of his, the authors Jaroslaw Iwaszkiewicz and Mieczyslaw Rytard. These two had just returned from the Podhale region, where they had spent their holidays making excursions into the surrounding area of Zakopane and Rabka. The young poets were practically bursting with enthusiasm for the mountains and the folklore of the Gorale. Eventually, they succeeded in infecting Szymanowski with their enthusiasm, too. The project of a Gorale ballet cropped up in their discussions, with both poets taking it on themselves to work out a scenario.

After his return from the second trip to America, the composer went to Zakopane for a prolonged period to collect material for his ballet. He took part in numerous "musical delights" – as he called the evenings of Gorale entertainment with dancing and music which friends had arranged for him – and on these occasions covered whole pages of his musical notebook with interesting melodies. Impatiently he waited for the completion of the ballet scenario on which Rytard was now working with his wife, a native of Gorale, Helena Roj.

While engaged on the preparatory work for the ballet, which fired his imagination more and more, the composer did not, however, neglect to complete the opera *King Roger*, in spite of having become very bored with this theme.

It was not until 1923 that Szymanowski received the first draft of the ballet scenario and he immediately got down to composing. His work on the ballet continued until 1931, however. In other words, between the initial research of this work and its completion, lay a time-span of ten years. Meanwhile, the scenario was being subjected to various changes. Gradually the title of the ballet became established: *Harnasie*.†

The plot of the ballet was as follows: – It is a holiday. In the meadow, girls have gathered together, among them a young Gorale girl, who is engaged to a rich *gazda*†† and is very beautiful. She is feeling sad because her parents want her to marry a man she does not love. Suddenly the firing of a shot can be heard – robbers appear on the scene. They have come down from the mountains to amuse themselves with the girls. The young robber chief (the Harnas) and the farmer's fiancée ignite with love for each other at first sight. The subsequent action takes place inside a Gorale hut where we witness the ceremonial putting-on of head-dresses. In the midst of the wedding dance, the robbers burst into the room. In the general commotion the light goes out, the Harnas snatches the bride and carries her off into the mountains.

The music of the ballet *Harnasie* presents us with a virtually pure extract of Gorale folklore. During his years in Zakopane—which had become his new home now that he had lost Timoshovka—Szymanowski adopted the Gorale culture and assimilated it intellectually in all its manifestations. In the score for *Harnasie*, which he constantly revised, he succeeded in emphasizing the peculiar characteristics of Podhale music: its ruggedness, its rhythmic vigor, the frenzy of its dances, and the broad breadth of its melodies. Szymanowski presented this entirely independent, undoubtedly exotic musical world by means of contemporary musical methods and made it accessible to the musical perception of all mankind.*

While working on the ballet, Szymanowski set himself an ambitious, if

*See page 84 for music examples 18, 19 and 20.

†In Polish "harnas" means "robber chief," "harnasie" plural, refers to robbers in the High Tatra, it implies the Gorale robbers who take from the rich and give to the poor.
††Among the Gorales, a *gazda* is a farm-owner.

45

artistically somewhat daring, task: to freshen up the form of the mazurka.

After all, it looked as if, after the mazurkas by Chopin, no one would ever achieve originality again in this genre. The countless mazurkas written by different composers usually turned out to be nothing more than imitations of Chopin originals. All Szymanowski took from Chopin's mazurkas was their general schema, into which, with great skill, he then poured a new musical content.

He did not, like Chopin, look to the folk-music of Masowia for the themes of his mazurkas, but to Podhale music, which by now had become so familiar to him. This cross between a lowland dance and Gorale melody produced some startling effects.

Szymanowski's Mazurkas clearly possess their own artistic profile, and this is not merely because of their Gorale themes, which, incidentally, were not used in all his mazurkas. The composer knew how to produce a special harmonic atmosphere and to develop a wealth of ideas. Like Chopin's mazurkas, every one of the Twenty Mazurkas, op. 50, by Szymanowski presents a unique musical individuality. These mazurkas also resulted in the clarification of Szymanowski's piano music, which here differs considerably from the dense masses of sound that characterize *Masks* and the Piano Sonata no. 3.*

The manuscript of Szymanowski's
The Visiting Soldier.

*See page 85 for music examples 21 and 22.

Artistic Maturity

Within a few years just after World War I, Szymanowski finally entered the period of complete mastery. On the numerous journeys to the West, which allowed him to acquaint himself with the situation of European post-war music, his personal, new style finally took shape, as did the most important basic principles of his new artistic ideology. All the changes that were taking place within him at this time were of the greatest significance, since they would affect all his future creations.

Szymanowski was approaching his forties by this time. Compared with other prominent composers of his generation, it might appear that he attained his artistic maturity fairly late in life. Ravel, Stravinsky, Falla, Bartók had all secured a place for themselves in the musical world by the time they were his age. Apart from differences in the type of talent, a certain amount of delay in Szymanowski's development was undoubtedly due to the fact that he had not had the same opportunities at the outset. The other composers were able to start their creative work simply by building on the achievements of the previous generation. Szymanowski, however, had had nothing to build on.

At the time when Szymanowski's career as a composer began, Polish musical composition was not keeping abreast with European music. What was more, it was adopting a positively rejective, if not hostile attitude towards the new trends. Throughout his life Szymanowski suffered badly from the consequences of this retrogressive way of thinking. It took up a great deal of his energy to ward off the attacks by conservative circles of the musical world. What made his position even more difficult was that he was forced to brave these attacks alone. It was not until 1930 that a young generation of Polish composers appeared which took it upon itself to fight some of the battles about the new Polish music. This is one of the most influential factors in the development of Szymanowski's creativity, and we must bear it in mind when we look at his frequent and seemingly impulsive changes in style.

Szymanowski's compositional activity fell into a time of radical change as far as European music was concerned. Already at the very beginning of his career, he found himself caught between different artistic trends which were all antagonistic to one another. At that time the major trends in music were less apparent than they now seem to us from a certain historical distance.

The young Szymanowski failed to comprehend that one and a half centuries of German musical dominance were just coming to an end and the center of progress was shifting to France. Among Polish composers of the older generation he found no leader who could make it easier for him to find his bearings in this forest of differing artistic watchwords. No wonder then that, having only himself to rely on, he kept getting lost and changing the direction of his creative work until he had finally found his way.

The strength Szymanowski had to muster in order to work his way through to the European music of his time was tremendous. However, it did not benefit just him but also the whole of future Polish music. Young Polish composers no longer needed to put all their energy into path-breaking as he had to, but could simply begin with Szymanowski.

One characteristic consequence of the new artistic ideology he had worked out for himself during the post-war period was his affiliation to Frederic Chopin. In him he now saw the ideal of a national composer, and he arrived at the conclusion that a natural evolution of Polish music could proceed only within the framework of the Chopin tradition. In an article published in the journal *Skamander*, Szymanowski wrote: "Frederic Chopin is a permanent example of what Polish music can be like, as well as one of the greatest symbols of a Europeanized Poland which loses none of its racial particularities and has climbed to the highest level of European culture."

We may well ask ourselves why Szymanowski reached this conclusion so late, since he was already quite clearly affiliated to Chopin in his Preludes op. 1. Why did he stray from this path again and start to look to German music for his models? Once again we must seek the answer in the Polish musical situation encountered by Szymanowski at the start of his compositional activities. If he refused to conform to its conservative direction, and if he had the ambition to attain the highest European standard in his own creations, then he had to turn resolutely away from everything that Polish composers of his time stood for. We already know that at that time he was against any folk element in music, dismissing it as a mere semblance of national music. In the same way, he had to reject anything that in Polish music at that time was considered a furtherance of Chopin's work, since any "affiliation" to Chopin in those days was in reality just a superficial imitation of some of his stylistic characteristics. Understandably, then, the path of least resistance held no temptation for Szymanowski.

Frederic Chopin.

At this point, however, circumstances were fundamentally different. Szymanowski approached Chopin as an already mature artist who disposes of a rich arsenal of compositional means. He now felt strong enough to continue where Chopin left off, and not to imitate.

In his beautiful work on Chopin,† Szymanowski stresses the necessity for a rediscovery of Chopin's works. "We state boldly," he writes there, "that despite all the uncritical, almost religious cult that has grown up around this national hero, he has never had full recognition as a great Polish artist. As a result of this, his inestimable work remained infertile, an isolated work, virtually on the fringe of subsequent Polish musical creation. But the work of a great artist ceases to be a perpetual source of living, creative power unless it is allowed to occupy its proper position in the national cultural consciousness—a perfectly clear position devoid of all sentimentality (. . .) Undoubtedly the most vital task for the future Young Poland in Music, a task on which its continued existence more or less depends, is the (. . .) renewed 'discovery' of Frederic Chopin, the final liberation of his mummy from the wrappings of all kinds of emotional rhetoric which have been piling up over the last century or so, the real and practical bringing-to-awareness of the paths that will lead Polish music to independence, paths which since Chopin no one has been able or willing to tread. . ." This is the exact explanation for Szymanowski's new artistic ideology.

The sudden change in Szymanowski's creative work after his return to Poland took him completely away from the impressionist style that characterized what he wrote during World War I. Some of these works—such as the Symphony no. 1, the Violin Concerto no. 1, and the String Quartet no. 1—he now heard for the first time. He also turned his attention to the mammoth score of his opera *King Roger*, the only work which forms a link with the war years long since past. The fame he now began to acquire abroad was based mainly on his works from that period. A special role in this respect was played both by *Myths* and the First Violin Concerto, works with an original style that turned out to be of astonishing novelty in contemporary violin literature.

One important event in Szymanowski's life—apart from the two trips to

†K. Szymanowski: "Fryderyk Chopin" in the monthly journal *Skamander*, 1923, Nos. 28-30.

**Szymanowski with Stefan Spiess
and Grzegorz Fitelberg in France
in 1922.**

Karol Szymanowski in 1927.

America which, as we know, in spite of Arthur Rubinstein's substantial support did not produce the expected results—was the concert of his works given in Paris in May 1922. This concert, organized by the well-known musical journal *Revue Musicale*, consolidated Szymanowski's position in the artistic circles of Paris. After Berlin and Vienna, Paris now became the main destination of the composer's foreign trips. Here performances of his works were given from time to time, and from here he observed the development of contemporary music in Europe.

Connected with Paris is the history of the origin of the most important of Szymanowski's sacred works, his *Stabat Mater*. In 1924, the Princess Polignac commissioned from him a work for soloists, choir, and orchestra which was to be given its premiere at one of her private concerts. Szymanowski hit upon the idea of composing a "peasant requiem," and turned to Jaroslaw Iwaszkiewicz for the adaptation of a suitable text.

As already indicated by the title alone, this work too would seem to have sprung from Szymanowski's interest in folklore at that time. But the tragic death of the composer's niece, Alusia Bartoszewicz, in January 1925 interrupted further work on the requiem. Szymanowski—like, incidentally, numerous European composers before him—succumbed to the charm of the medieval fast-sequence which, with moving simplicity, sings about the sufferings of the mother of God at the foot of the cross.*

Despite its entirely modern character, the music of *Stabat Mater* clearly exhibits archaic features. In this work, allusions to medieval music can repeatedly be heard, discreetly intimated in the melodic line or the combination of chords. Above all, however, the music of *Stabat Mater* bears the character of folk-music, although quotations from folklore are absent here. We are confronted with a national quality similar to that of *Slopiewnie*.

The fact that for his composition Szymanowski chose the Polish transcription of the sequence and not its original Latin text, had its deep-seated reasons. In the comments on *Stabat Mater* which the composer published in a musical journal we read: "I may be mistaken, but I am under the impression that, even for people who know Latin very well, this language has lost its emotional content and preserved only the conceptual content (. . .). this is because Latin has lost its direct contact with life and has—while, of course, remaining sublime—become a frozen form of language. I confess contritely that perhaps for this reason a 'Swiety Boze' sung somewhere in a tiny little village church or my beloved 'Gorzkie zale'†—every word of which is a poetically living organism to me—arouses the religious instinct inside me a hundred times more strongly than a Latin mass, be it ever so ingenious."

In other words, only the living contents of the Sequence for Lent which Jozef Jankowski†† had extracted from the frozen wrappings of the Latin words were able to stimulate Szymanowski's creative imagination. Perhaps this also explains why the composer never brought himself to write a Latin mass, in spite of toying with the idea for a considerable time.

In the period after the War, we detect only a slight interest in lyrical poetry, which until then had formed the basis for a significant proportion of his compositions. After *Slopiewnie*, the *Children's Rhymes*, op. 49, constituted his next collection of songs. They were composed during the years 1922-1923.

These songs are distinguished by their unusual charm. The composer knew how to re-create the atmosphere of a nursery in which two little girls—Lalka and Krysia—make up simple rhymes about animals, stars, the daughter of a king, and about the holy Christine, who did not have a mother. By means of very simple,

*See pages 86-87 for music example 23 and page 87 for music example 24.

†"Swiety Boze" ("Holy God") and "Gorzkie zale" ("Bitter Laments") are popular national hymns used throughout the Catholic Church in Poland. The former is occasionally sung in difficult or dangerous times, the second regularly on Sundays in Lent.

††Author of the Polish translation of *Stabat Mater* which Szymanowski set to music. The work can also be performed with the original Latin words.

uncontrived musical techniques, Szymanowski portrayed both the naiveté and the seriousness with which the girls treat the heroes of their poems. These *Children's Rhymes* by Szymanowski are twenty short lyrical masterpieces which easily hold their own alongside the famous cycle *The Nursery* by Modest Musorgsky. *

The *Children's Rhymes* were followed by a prolonged break in Szymanowski's composition of songs. Until 1927, which constituted another decisive turning-point in the life of Szymanowski, just a few shorter works were written.

In July 1925, while staying at the summer resort Saint-Jean-de-Luz, where he had been invited by his friend Dorothy Jordan-Robinson, he composed a piece for violin and piano with the title "La Berceuse d'Aïtacho Enia" ("d'Aïtacho Enia" was the name of the villa belonging to Mrs. Robinson). This lullaby ranks among the most heartfelt of Szymanowski's compositions. The music is simple, almost austere in its sparse use of expressive techniques.

From the same year originates the second piece of music Szymanowski wrote for the stage, his incidental music for Act Five of the tragedy *Prince Potemkin* by Tadeus Micinski. Also from this period stem comprehensive notes on a piano concerto which unfortunately was never written.

In 1926, Szymanowski composed *Four Polish Dances* for piano: a mazurka, a krakowiak (or cracovienne), an oberek, and a polonaise. These had been commissioned by an English publishing company (Oxford University Press) for a collection of dances from different countries.

The manuscript of *Stabat Mater*.

52   *See pages 87-89 for music example 25.

The Teacher and Pedagogue

The Senate of the Warsaw Music Academy, where Szymanowski was a rector from 1930 to 1932.

In the course of his compositional work in revived Poland, Szymanowski became, for the entire young generation of Polish musicians, the leading figure, the embodiment of renewal and of progress in Polish music. This position was further strengthened by the battle he fought in the press in defense of his artistic ideology. All of musical youth crowded around him, and Szymanowski, although not officially a teacher, was most willing to serve the young people, to let them derive benefit from his experience and his knowledge, and to point them in the right direction where their musical development was concerned.

He became increasingly conscious of the fact that young composers should not be held back by such obstacles as had once made his own artistic development much more difficult and had, in fact, delayed it. Once he had succeeded in breaking down the main barriers, the young generation was to continue building and not to struggle with ghosts from the past. Only then would the growth of contemporary Polish music begin, and that was what mattered to him.

It was not enough for him, however, to speak through his musical works and aesthetic treatises. Personal contact with young composers was essential. All the signs were that sooner or later he would be forced into some teaching activity.

Szymanowski's attitude to the question as to whether or not composition should be taught also underwent an interesting evolution. For a long time, he dismissed any instruction in this field as pointless. He felt that if a pupil had a genuine creative gift, his artistic development would only be hindered by the individuality of his composition teacher, who would, after all, need to be a good composer himself. It is very likely that Szymanowski's own adverse experiences on the road to acquiring musical knowledge led him to form this attitude.

In one of his notebooks, Szymanowski jotted down some fairly bitingly formulated sentences on the teaching of composition: "I believe it was Darwin who said that all those working as scientists could be divided into the self-taught and the know-nothings. How much truer this is with respect to the art world! One should add that the know-nothings are primarily those who have learnt the most at official schools of art. One can almost assert that someone's future position in the art world is determined by the degree of strength with which the creative instinct, the talent of the individual concerned, resists the immediate influence—i.e., the teaching methods—of the official professor."

Fortunately, Szymanowski was not doctrinaire. He was always prepared to change even a quite extreme opinion if, on deeper analysis, his reasoning turned out to have been at fault. In this case, too, he changed his mind once he realized that his participation in the instruction of young students of composition would help contemporary Polish music to catch up all the more quickly.

At the end of 1926, the Ministry of Education for the People approached Szymanowski with the suggestion that he take on the post of director at the Warsaw Conservatory. The composer remained undecided for a fairly long time. To take over from Henryk Melcer—who had been director for many years, had initiated a lot of improvements at the institute, and had recently resigned because of a conflict with the school-board—embarrassed him. Furthermore, Szymanowski was aware that a portion of the faculty was hostile towards him, which meant that he would have to overcome a great deal of resistance and opposition.

Acceptance of the offered post would also impose a restriction on his freedom of movement by tying him to Warsaw for the whole duration of the academic year—and Szymanowski liked travelling. Teaching at the conservatory would, further, cut down considerably on the time he was able to devote to his own creative work.

In this connection, it is worth mentioning a little-known episode. Almost simultaneously with the offer of the directorship at the Warsaw Conservatory, Szymanowski received an invitation to take on a similar post at the Cairo Conservatory. The Egyptian government had at that time decided to extend and re-organize the conservatory in Cairo. For the director's post they were seeking a prominent European composer who had already displayed an interest in oriental music in his compositions published so far. They had, in fact, turned to Joseph Marx—vice-chancellor of the Musical Academy of Vienna and an old friend of Szymanowski's—with the request to track down a suitable candidate. Marx naturally suggested above all Szymanowski, who completely satisfied all the conditions stipulated by the Egyptian government.

The offer was very tempting indeed. Szymanowski would have spent several months of the year in Egypt, in a climate which had always suited his weak lungs very well. Since the post would have earned him a fairly substantial income, he would have been able to devote the rest of the year to his compositions, without any material worries. To the astonishment of his friends, Szymanowski did not, however, accept the Egyptian offer but opted for Warsaw instead. His feeling of duty towards the musical culture of his own country predominated.

Szymanowski commenced teaching in March 1927. The history of this engagement is, however, among the most embarrassing proceedings in the Polish musical life of that time. From the moment the composer entered the Warsaw Conservatory building, there began a malicious battle against him which was not particular about its means of attack and pursued the goal of damaging his reputation both with the authorities and in society. Szymanowski parried the blows aimed at him with the delicacy and tact that were characteristic of him. He acted under the misconception that he would still succeed in reaching a compromise.

This indecisive behavior, of course, immediately turned against him. He made a total of two attempts to keep the reins of the Warsaw Conservatory in his hands, and twice he was forced to retreat under the pressure exerted by the opposition. The latter consisted of people who suspected that, in the progressive trend represented by Szymanowski, there was a deadly danger to their own creations, which were based on antiquated models.

A few days after taking up the directorship at the Warsaw Conservatory, Szymanowski, in an interview for a Warsaw newspaper, outlined his programme for the reform: "Of prime importance to me will be that the Conservatory become a custodian of musical culture in its highest sense. In accordance with my basic attitude, which regards the achievements of contemporary music as real and extraordinarily valuable, I shall, of course, take the latest results in this field into consideration. I fully acknowledge artistic traditionalism as a point of departure—a good musical nursery, as it were. However, our goal is not 'yesterday' but 'today' and 'tomorrow'—in other words, creation, not encapsulation in what has been achieved already." This, then, was the direction in which Szymanowski intended to lead the young generation of musicians.

Against this gentle pedagogic revolution, which was to rest mainly on the modernization of teaching methods and on acquainting the students not only with classical musical literature but also with works written in contemporary musical language, a whole campaign began to be mobilized. Szymanowski expended all his energy on defending the reform. Already at the end of 1928, he

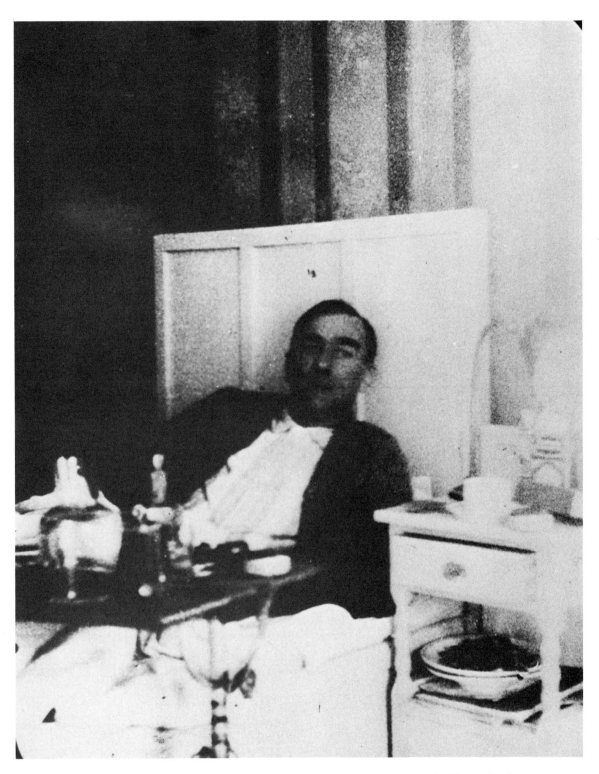

**Szymanowski at the Davos health
resort where he stayed from 1929
until May 1930.**

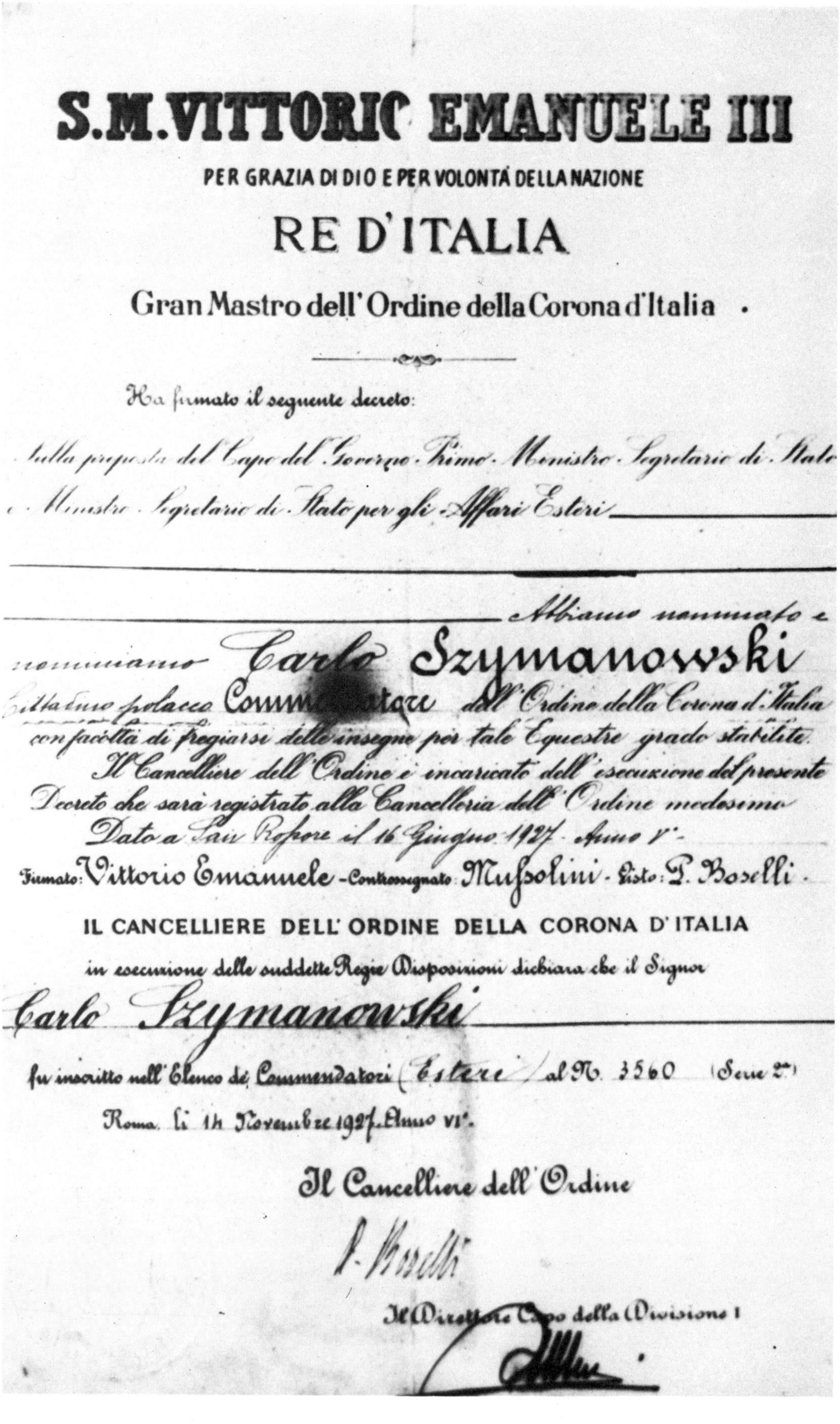

S.M.VITTORIO EMANUELE III
PER GRAZIA DI DIO E PER VOLONTÀ DELLA NAZIONE
RE D'ITALIA
Gran Mastro dell'Ordine della Corona d'Italia .

Ha firmato il seguente decreto:

sulla proposta del Capo del Governo Primo Ministro Segretario di Stato

e Ministro Segretario di Stato per gli Affari Esteri

Abbiamo nominato e nominiamo **Carlo Szymanowski**
cittadino polacco Commendatore dell'Ordine della Corona d'Italia
con facoltà di fregiarsi delle insegne per tale Equestre grado stabilite.
Il Cancelliere dell'Ordine è incaricato dell'esecuzione del presente
Decreto che sarà registrato alla Cancelleria dell'Ordine medesimo
Dato a San Rossore il 16 Giugno 1927. Anno V.
Firmato: Vittorio Emanuele - Controsegnato Mussolini - Visto: P. Boselli.

IL CANCELLIERE DELL'ORDINE DELLA CORONA D'ITALIA

in esecuzione delle suddette Regie Disposizioni dichiara che il Signor

Carlo Szymanowski

fu inscritto nell'Elenco dei Commendatori (Esteri) al N. 3560 (Serie 2ª)

Roma, li 14 Novembre 1927. Anno VI.

Il Cancelliere dell'Ordine

Il Direttore Capo della Divisione I

was forced to request leave of absence for health reasons. He went to Edlach in Austria to recuperate and spent two months there. In March 1929, he returned to his work at the Conservatory only to find an even worse situation than before his departure.

A few months later, he admitted defeat and handed in his resignation. "The last subjective experiences at the Conservatory made it absolutely clear to me that if I had waited another year, I would have been a complete internal wreck," he wrote to August Iwanski in July 1929. "Personally, I fear this may already have happened in any case, but one must never give up hope altogether (. . .) Since the fall, I have ceased to be director of the Conservatory (. . .). Believe me, it was not an easy decision to make (. . .). I regret all that terrible effort I put into the work. Nevertheless, I am confronted with the undoubted psychological fact: *aut−aut* ["either−or" in Latin], either the Conservatory or I. I cannot go on like this any longer."

The entire creative work produced by Szymanowski during the period of his directorship, i.e., the years 1927-1929, confined itself to one Vocalise-Etude which he wrote for the French publishing company Alphonse Leduc and *Six Songs from Kurpie*† for mixed chorus. We can see that Szymanowski's fears that he might not be able to combine the director's duties with his compositional work were fully justified.

The *Songs from Kurpie* are a particularly interesting work. After Podhale, Szymanowski turned his attention to the music of the Kurpie region. He became acquainted with this music through the collection *Wesele na Kurpiach (Kurpie Wedding)* by the clergyman Wladyslaw Skierkowski. With these songs, Szymanowski not only produced an exemplary adaptation of musical folklore, but also enriched Polish choral music with entirely new examples of choral treatment.

Having neither the time nor the energy for a more intense compositional activity, Szymanowski made plans for new works. He re-examined his earlier intention of writing an opera based on the tragedy *Klatwa (The Curse)* by Stanislaw Wyspianski. In Edlach he looked through the libretto *Eva spielt mit Puppen (Eva plays with dolls)* by Auerbach, which Universal Edition had recommended to him. Finally, however, he did not decide on any particular work.

A few days after the end of the academic year and after handing in his resignation at the Ministry of Education for the People, Szymanowski went to Edlach a second time to recuperate. He was under the mistaken impression that he would be able to regain his strength within a month, and would then at last get down to composing again. Instead of improving, however, his state of health began to get worse. On the advice of a nurse at the sanatorium where he was staying, he decided to go to Vienna for a thorough medical examination.

From Vienna, Szymanowski wrote to Janusz Miketta: "The whole month I was in Edlach, I was feeling very ill and had a temperature. The idiotic doctors there were no good at all, just talked about nerves and similar nonsense. At last, I came here, and after consultations and X-rays it turned out, of course, that the common Polish tuberculosis had got me in its grip. It had, in fact, reached a rather worrisome stage (particularly the right lung) and must have been with me for at least three or four months. As you can see, the honor of having had a directorship has cost me quite dearly!"

It was a catastrophic situation. Almost at the last moment when it was still possible to save him, he was admitted to the exemplary sanatorium "Guardaval" in Davos, Switzerland. Thanks to careful medical treatment and an excellent climate, the tuberculosis was kept in check. In the course of nine months, Szymanowski slowly recovered his health.

Condemned to long months of total isolation, he sank into reflections about problems which were forced upon him by his work at the Conservatory not all that long ago. He was passionately interested in the question of musical education. Now, away from the teaching staff at the Warsaw Conservatory who were

†"Kurpie" is the Polish name of a landscape and its inhabitants in Poland situated in the north of Masowia in the river basin of the Narew, around the villages of Ostroleka and Myszyniec. This region is rich in forests and a peculiar folk art of its own.

forever picking quarrels amongst themselves, he was able to grasp the implications of this important question much more easily. It was perfectly clear to him that in a country where music had been so neglected, it was not enough to extend this field upwards—even if composers and performing musicians were to receive the most modern form of education—but that musical culture had to grow above all in breadth, in society itself. As a result of these reflections, Davos saw the production of a clever and beautifully written pamphlet entitled "The Educational Role of Musical Culture in Society."

In it, Szymanowski analyzes the reasons for the indifference of the Polish state to matters of music, and comes to the conclusion that this springs from ignorance of the ethical effect of music: "It seemed as if the pre-war situation† was still prevailing where music was concerned, a situation in which music—once a mild narcotic used to reduce alertness in certain social classes—was treated as a dessert which in times of grim battles for the daily bread of the nation's political existence was not worth worrying about. What was forgotten at that time was the fact that music is a powerful weapon in the battle against the ignorance and barbarism of the masses, a genuine food for the intellect, with undoubtedly the greatest amount of life-giving vitamins which most readily penetrate into the deepest layers of society (. . .). It seems almost a paradox or, worse still, the sign of a completely naive social idealism that I stubbornly go on talking about music—about what appears to be the most abstract game of our imagination and the one furthest removed from life—almost as of a panacea that heals the most painful of social wounds. Nevertheless I shall go on maintaining, with equal stubbornness, that while music may not be a panacea, it is yet one of the best medicines, for its effect is by no means as much of an abstraction as would appear, because, among all the fine arts, music possesses in the purest degree the astonishing gift of instantly releasing the creative instinct, an instinct which actually is the only possible psychological attitude to the pure fact of life."

Karol Szymanowski and Artur Taube in Davos in 1930.

It goes without saying that, in accordance with what he had written about the ethical effect of music, the demands Szymanowski made on musicians were very high. The latter were expected "in their consciousness to combine the deep love for, and conviction of the sublime majesty of, true art with the feeling of social responsibility for it."

Szymanowski dedicated this work to Janusz Miketta, a man who until the last moment of his life fought for new ways to achieve progress in the musical culture of Poland.

While Szymanowski was still staying in Davos, the atmosphere at the Warsaw Conservatory had already been somewhat purified thanks to the energetic efforts of Janusz Miketta, who was inspector of music schools at that time. Furthermore, in conjunction with the reform in musical education which was carried out in Poland during that period, the institute was elevated to the level of a musical college with the rights of an academy. The only candidate suitable for the post of rector at this college was, of course, Szymanowski.

Having returned home in May 1930, the composer devoted himself with renewed vigor to the service of the first academy of music in Poland, in the hope that this time it would be possible for the reformatory work to be completed. The festive opening of the Academy was to take place in November, and Szymanowski undertook to compose a "Veni Creator" (after words by Stanislaw Wyspianski) especially for this ceremony.

Szymanowski spent the whole summer of that year in Zakopane, which he had chosen as his permanent place of residence. Thanks to the successful treatment received in Davos, his creative powers had been fully restored to him. His life now entered the last phase of intense compositional activity. During July and August, he composed "Veni Creator" and started drafting music to the words of the *Litany* by Jerzy Liebert. He also returned to his work on the score for *Harnasie*, which had been awaiting its final completion for some years.

†The time before World War I when Poland was divided up into three regions, all of which were annexed to foreign powers.

Szymanowski's *Doctor Honoric Causa* diploma.

Q. F. F. F. Q. S.

SUMMIS AUSPICIIS

SERENISSIMAE REIPUBLICAE POLONORUM

NOS

EDMUNDUS ZAŁĘSKI

AGRI PLANTARUMQUE CULTURAE PROFESSOR P. O.
S. C. UNIVERSITATIS IAGELLONICAE RECTOR MAGNIFICUS

ET

ROMANUS DYBOSKI

PHILOSOPHIAE DR. HISTORIAE LITTERARUM ANGLICARUM PROFESSOR P. O.
S. C. ORDINIS PHILOSOPHORUM DECANUS

IN

VIRUM ILLUSTRISSIMUM

CAROLUM SZYMANOWSKI

ORIUNDUM TYMOSZOWKA IN UKRAINA
S. C. RECTOREM SCHOLAE MUSICAE SUPERIORIS VARSOVIENSIS QUOD CONSERVATORIUM PUBLICUM APPELLATUR,
MODORUM MUSICORUM FACTOREM.
QUI INGENIUM MUSICUM A NATURA SIBI DATUM ASSIDUO LABORE MAXIMAQUE VOLUNTATIS MENTISQUE
CONTENTIONE MIRUM QUANTUM EXCOLUIT CONFIRMAVITQUE MULTISQUE OPERIBUS VARIORUM GENERUM
DIVERSARUMQUE FORMARUM PER SEX LUSTRA COMPOSITIS HUIUS SAECULI INGENIUM OPTIME EXPRESSIT
NOVASQUE VIAS MUSICIS PROMOVENDIS APERUIT; QUI ET IPSE SEMPER AD SUMMA ARTIS FASTIGIA TETENDIT
ET AUDIENTIUM ANIMOS SENSUSQUE SECUM AD ALTISSIMA CORRIPUIT. ITA UT NOMINIS SUI GLORIA MERITISSIMO
APUD OMNES GENTES PARTA NOVUM MUSICAE POLONAE ADDERET SPLENDOREM.

DOCTORIS PHILOSOPHIAE

HONORIS CAUSA

NOMEN ET DIGNITATEM, IURA ET PRIVILEGIA CONTULIMUS IN EIUSQUE REI FIDEM HASCE LITTERAS UNIVERSITATIS
SIGILLO SANCIENDAS CURAVIMUS.

DABAMUS CRACOVIAE, DIE XII MENSIS DECEMBRIS A. D. MCMXXX.

RECTOR   DECANUS

It was not until the fall that Szymanowski had to give up composing in order to get down to a literary task which occupied him no less intensely, for this year there were two ceremonies awaiting him for which it was customary to prepare appropriate speeches. In November, he took on the post as rector at the musical academy. In his inaugural address, he pointed to Frederic Chopin as the only sublime model for every Polish musician, describing him as the one who "until the end of the sad days of his short life spoke, with unflinching steadfastness and firm belief, to the whole world – in the universally comprehensible and the most beautiful language in the world, the language of his music – of the strength, indestructibility, and depth of the Polish creative genius."

In December, Szymanowski travelled to Cracow to take part in the ceremony of the bestowal of an honorary doctorate at the Jagiello University. This honor, which among musicians had theretofore been bestowed only on Ignacy Paderewski, gave him real pleasure. The professor conferring the degree was Zdzislaw Jachimecki. All in all, the year 1930 was probably the happiest in Szymanowski's life, allowing him as it did – albeit for only a short time – to enjoy his well-being to the full.

Already the following year was a less happy one. He managed only to complete *Harnasie*, then he was once again caught up in the arguments between supporters and opponents of the musical academy. Again, he himself was singled out as the main target. The former opposition once more prepared for an all-out attack. No stone was left unturned; the lack of orientation in matters of art on the part of various eminent personalities was exploited. In short, nothing was left untried to wreck the institute even before it had completed its germination. This time, however, Szymanowski could not afford to risk his health again by putting too much energy into the defense. When he had become convinced that there was no hope of a favorable solution, he tendered his resignation. In February 1932, he gave up his position as rector and never returned to teaching again.

Today, looking from a more or less historical perspective at the sad story of Szymanowski's struggle to raise the standards of Polish musical schools, we can see clearly that it was not only the composer who was wronged here, but also – and above all – the whole of Polish musical culture. It should be a matter of course that if the most prominent musical authority – and this Szymanowski was beyond question – is prepared to take on the directorship of the most important musical college in Poland and personally to supervise the musical education of the young, everyone should be duty-bound to help and support him in this task. Here, on the other hand, this important matter came to grief because of personal altercations, questions of jurisdiction, and intrigues. Even the then Ministry for the Education of the People – a body with responsibility for the development of natural culture – calmly looked on as Szymanowski invested his last shred of energy in the battles against obscurantism in music, for progress in the field of musical education!

Luckily, despite the short duration of his career as a pedagogue, Szymanowski knew how to fire the imagination of every one of the more talented students at the Conservatory. The young refused to be betrayed, and their healthy instinct told them that the path indicated by Szymanowski was the one that led to genuine progress. And, thanks to this handful of students, Szymanowski's work was not completely in vain. Although the composer had to suffer defeat as a rector, he did not do the same as a teacher, and he was able to look forward to the future of Polish music with optimism.

In an interview granted to the author Michal Choromanski (*Wiadomosci Literackie*, 1932, No. 461), we read the following: "It is important that these young people be allowed to have their say. They are not just gifted but also have initiative and, finally, a sense of modern reality. And they know very well for what purpose I 'disorganized' the state conservatory for a number of years. Then there will come the rehabilitation of all my work and my efforts, which today seem fruitless and lost forever."

Facing page: Szymanowski receiving the title of *Doctor Honoris Causa.*

Szymanowski and Kochanski in Zakopane.

The Final Years

Divested of all offices and honors, Szymanowski returned to Zakopane, to the villa "Atma"† which today has already become historical. With a greater zeal than ever, he got down to composing. "With tragic shadows on the pale brow," he joked in conversation with Michal Choromanski, "a real *Rector Magnificus in partibus infidelium,* given back unto his home like Cincinnatus, I simultaneously returned to that which is after all my most important duty. Less than six months have passed since my exodus, and I have already completed one symphony, one violin concerto, several drafts, and new ideas."

1932 was in fact a very productive year for Szymanowski. Above all he finished the *Songs from Kurpie* for solo voice with piano accompaniment. *

For it was at this time that further small volumes of *Puszcza kurpiowska w piesni* (The Kurpie forest in song) by Wladyslaw Skierkowski were published, in which the peculiar beauty of the music of the Kurie forests was already fully revealed. Szymanowski liked to change the region of his interest in folklore, the more so since his "discovery" of Podhale music had precipitated an "infectious" Gorale music fashion among young composers. Following his example, mazurkas of the Podhale variety were shooting up everywhere like mushrooms, a fact which he actually found quite irritating.

It is also at this time that Szymanowski went back to his plans to write an opera. He invited Iwaszkiewicz to his house in Zakopane, and together they searched for an interesting subject for an opera. Szymanowski suggested the *Memoirs* by Benvenuto Cellini or "The King's Coat" by Andersen and Iwaszkiewicz opted for the latter's "Flight to Bagdad." Ultimately they settled for none of these.

Parallel with the *Songs from Kurpie* developed the score for the Symphony no. 4. This work forms a link between the symphony and piano concerto genres. It is in fact a "Sinfonia concertante." The piano plays a dual role in this piece: in places it acts as the dominant solo instrument; elsewhere it frequently has to submit to other instruments. The piano part of the Symphony no. 4 is very difficult indeed, having been written by Szymanowski with the intention that he would be executing it himself. It evolved from his own individual piano-playing technique, the elements of which are not always comfortable for other pianists.

The most effective movement of the Fourth Symphony is the final allegro, which represents a stylization of the Kujawiak.†† When working on this composition, Szymanowski made use of his earlier drafts for a piano concerto. The introductory theme brought in by the piano at the beginning of the concerto had also been taking shape in his mind over a considerable time. Already in 1927, Szymanowski had demonstrated it to Arthur Rubinstein, who responded by improvising a whole cycle of variations on it on the spot.**

After completing the Fourth Symphony in June 1932, Szymanowski went to Paris, where he participated in a festival of Polish music, which lasted for several days and which had been organized with a lot of help from Paderewski. On his return journey from Paris, he was accompanied by Pawel Kochanski, who per-

Szymanowski in front of his Atma home, a mountain cabin he rented in 1930 and where he lived after that. The mountain peoples' folklore always had a fascination for him.

†This house, built in the Gorale style, accommodates the Szymanowski Museum.

††This is an old Polish peasant dance—in three-four time, with a mazurka-type rhythm—from the Kujawy region, the countryside surrounding the towns of Inowroclaw and Wloclawek.

*See page 89 for music example 26; **see page 90 for music example 27.

suaded him to write a new violin concerto.

Within four weeks, the composer had drafted the entire Violin Concerto no. 2. "Pawel provoked me into writing it, and has practically squeezed the whole (second) violin concerto out of me," the composer complained in a letter to Zygmunt Mycielski. After Kochanski had departed, Szymanowski slowly orchestrated the concerto. The score was not completed until September of the following year.

Kochanski, who wanted to extend the concerto to half an hour's duration, composed a longish cadenza for it. The Violin Concerto no. 2, which contains themes with elements of Podhale folk-music in them, is Szymanowski's last great work.[*]

The premiere of the concerto turned out to be the occasion of the two friends' final farewell. Kochanski, to whose energy we owe the existence of this work, became seriously ill. Despite great physical weakness, he decided to go ahead with the performance of the concerto rather than disappoint the composer. The premiere took place on October 6th, 1933, at the Warsaw Philharmonia. The conductor was Grzegorz Fitelberg. This was the last performance ever given by the great violinist. After returning to America, Kochanski died in New York in January of the following year.

While displaying his creative powers to the full, Szymanowski was suddenly confronted with the ghost of that dangerous illness he had once before conquered in Davos. As a result of his resignation from the director's post at the Warsaw Conservatory, the composer's material situation had, unfortunately, worsened too. Apart from a certain amount of financial assistance which, since his treatment in Davos, he had been receiving regularly from America (thanks to the efforts of Kochanski's wife Zofia), he had to rely exclusively on earnings from his compositions. However, although numerous compositions of his were being performed both in Poland and abroad, his income from this source was minimal. That was why a repetition of the expensive treatment at a Swiss sanatorium was out of the question this time.

To improve his financial situation, Szymanowski began to prepare himself for the role of concert pianist, and it was for this purpose that he wrote his Symphony no. 4. From 1933, he performed at concerts all over Europe, which served to consolidate his reputation considerably. It also improved his material position insofar as he had money when he travelled and played. Conversely, during the summer months, when no concerts were given anywhere, the inhabitants of the house "Atma" in Zakopane suffered genuine hardship. Worst of all, however, the strenuous concert tours caused a serious deterioration in his health. Many people today still remember their sad encounters with Szymanowski on various European routes when, weakened by illness, he managed only by a tremendous effort of will to drag himself from one concert to another.

Needless to say, he had very little energy left for composing. After having written his Violin Concerto no. 2, he was no longer able to rise to another work of the same dimensions. Over a period of two years, he drafted a Concertino for Piano and Orchestra, with which he wanted to replace his Fourth Symphony in the concert programmes. He managed to complete only the first movement, however. The rest never got beyond the draft-stage. During the uprising in Warsaw in 1944, this composition, together with the manuscript collection of the National Library, became a victim of the flames.

Szymanowski's final work is Two Mazurkas, op. 62, which were composed at the end of 1934 for Sir Victor Cazalet. They were commissioned by this rich music-lover during one of Szymanowski's visits to London. Their first-ever performance was given—by the composer—at a private concert at Cazalet's house.

In the difficult circumstances that governed Szymanowski's final years of life, his increasing success abroad was the only positive thing. Until about 1928, Szymanowski was known outside Poland mainly as the composer of *Myths* and the First Violin Concerto, i.e., the works which had found such excellent interpreters in Pawel Kochanski and Bronislaw Huberman. In 1929, after the per-

Left to Right: **Zofia Szymanowska, Krystyna Grzybowska, Karol Szymanowski, Pawel Kochanski and Emil Mlynarski on the porch of Villa Atma.**

*See page 90 for music example 28.

**Szymanowski with the Krakow
Orchestra in 1929.**

The composer with his sister
Stanislawa (Davos, 1930).

formance in Poznan, the *Stabat Mater* began its triumphal procession through Europe and was received with admiration everywhere.

Various establishments now also started to take an interest in Szymanowski's earlier works. For instance, in October 1932, the Narodni Divadlo in Prague gave a very successful performance of his *King Roger*. At more or less the same time, his Symphony no. 4 was performed at a number of concerts. The premiere had taken place in Poznan. Subsequently the work passed through all the musical centers of Europe. Together with Fitelberg, who had from the early stages of his friend's career as a composer faithfully devoted himself to the promotion of his symphonic works, Szymanowski performed this work more than thirty times between 1932 and 1935.

The Symphony no. 4 was followed by the ballet *Harnasie*. This was first performed in Prague in May 1935, then in Paris in April 1936. In Poland, alas, there was no incentive for a production of this work until after the composer's death.

The Parisian premiere of *Harnasie* was to be the composer's last great triumph. The ballet was given a very meticulous performance, with the excellent dancer Serge Lifar in the leading role. It met with sweeping success. "As for myself," wrote Szymanowski in one of his letters after the premiere, "apart from the fact that I am very tired and without money, everything is marvellous for the moment. I received much praise, *Harnasie* is much talked about and flatteringly so. Ninety percent of the reviews are excellent, and those ten percent of fault-finders are no more than was to be expected. In fact, things would be even worse if they did not exist."

Karol Szymanowski's favorite room at Atma.

The two months Szymanowski spent in Paris in connection with the production of *Harnasie* helped him to regain his strength, thanks to the atmosphere of excitement caused by his success. Amidst the continuing elation due to further performances of the ballet, amidst official receptions, banquets, and festivities, it looked as if the disease which had weakened his constitution more and more had now met with defeat after all. However, after having left Paris, Szymanowski suddenly felt worse than ever before. He should really have returned to southern France, to Grasse, where he had already been staying from January to March on his doctor's recommendation. Unfortunately, his funds had been seriously depleted by the Paris festivities and, instead of being able to go to Grasse, he had to return to Poland. As the tuberculosis of the larynx had progressed, the doctors did not permit him to go to Zakopane for the summer. He, therefore, spent that season in the close and dusty city of Warsaw.

Everything, in fact, went tragically wrong during this final period. That Szymanowski was seriously ill had become common knowledge, nor was it a secret to any of his relatives and friends that he had no money to go away for treatment. As a matter of fact, a special committee was formed in Warsaw – consisting of representatives of the civil service and the business world – which was to organize charitable aid for the composer. Ultimately, however, this resulted in more trouble and actual embarrassment than money. Furthermore, every so often optimistic rumors were spread among the circle of his acquaintances that his condition was not so serious after all, and for this reason the committee did not come to his aid.

Thus, Szymanowski spent the whole summer of 1936 within the hot walls of Warsaw. Subsequently he also endured the wet fall weather in this environment, and it was not until November that he was able to travel to France for further treatment.

After a short stay in Paris, visiting his trusted doctor, who also regarded his state of health with optimism, Szymanowski went on to Grasse, where he stayed in solitude at a hotel. Because he was receiving only a very modest allowance which was supposed to pay for his treatment, he was not able to employ a permanent nurse. He had to endure agonizing pain and discomfort. Because the disease affected the whole of his oral cavity, he was able neither to eat nor speak. In the letters he sent home, he tried to sound cheerful, because he did not want his family to worry about him.

Szymanowski tried hard to fight his illness. He had a pianino brought to his room, and intended to start work on a new ballet called *Ulysses' Return Home*. "The mere possibility of a composition will have a beneficial effect on my frame of mind," he wrote to his secretary Leonia Gradstein, "and, besides, it would really be worthwhile to write something new! I have not really composed anything for the last couple of years."

Unfortunately, however, he was no longer able to compose. In January 1937, he wrote to his secretary: "If only I could conquer this terrible apathy I feel and do some work. Then, I think, I would somehow regain my equilibrium. But just think! After so many years – at first these concerts, then the illness! In such circumstances even the shoemaker forgets how to make shoes! Yesterday I began to busy myself with my earlier pieces – pretending I had been 'working on them'!"

The only letter in which the composer openly describes his condition is addressed to Jaroslaw Iwaszkiewicz. But even there the illness is mentioned only by the way, so that we, if we read the letter and know what happened subsequently, can only now understand fully that disaster was already inevitable.

"The real reason for my depression," wrote Szymanowski, "is my conviction that my (physical) condition is getting worse all the time. And that is, in fact, what is happening. I am no longer able to speak at all, eating I find very difficult and am therefore losing weight. I do not write this to anyone, for fear the news might get to my ladies – and this vast distance would, of course, heighten their anxiety still more. I, therefore, beg of you to keep this to yourself. I intend to stay here for a little longer. If there should not be a change for the better, I shall presumably return to Paris to have some sort of operation (some sort of cauterization) as a last resort. This operation is supposed to produce excellent results . . ."

Szymanowski with costume designer Irena Lorentowicz and ballet dancer Serge Lifar in Paris in 1935.

Eventually the sick man felt he could endure his sufferings no more. Szymanowski decided to summon his secretary – Leonia Gradstein – to his side. By this time it was already March 1937. No sooner had Miss Gradstein arrived in Grasse than she became aware of the terrible situation. She immediately arranged for the composer to be transferred to a sanatorium and notified his family. Szymanowski was first taken to Cannes and from there to Lausanne, to the sanatorium of Dr. Dufour.

However, as it turned out, help had arrived too late. In the course of those few months which the sick man had spent in Grasse without medical treatment, the tuberculosis had completely destroyed his lung tissue and the oral cavity.

On March 29th, 1937, fifteen minutes after midnight, Karol Szymanowski died. His sister Stanislawa was present in the hour of his death.

The first to place a floral wreath on the composer's coffin was Ignacy Paderewski.

The news of the great composer's death came as a complete shock to the Polish people. Even his closest friends had not been prepared for this catastrophe.

Szymanowski was given a magnificent funeral at the public's expense. The embalmed body was transferred to Warsaw where part of the obsequies took place. His heart was removed and was to be laid to rest in the Church of the Cross next to the heart of Chopin. Unfortunately this was not to happen and the composer's poor heart was burnt during the Warsaw uprising in 1944.

The coffin was removed from Warsaw to Cracow and buried there on April 7th, 1937, in the Heroes' Crypt on the Skalka.

Above: The composer is mourned in Krakow. *Below:* The funeral of Karol Szymanowski.

Karol Szymanowski.

Postscript

by H. P. Anders

In the first half of the twentieth century, there was no greater composer in Poland than Karol Szymanowski (1882-1937). The wonderful lyricism of his First Violin Concerto, the original, powerful, gripping rhythms of the folk-tunes in his ballet *Harnasie*, the deeply moving lament of the melodies in his *Stabat Mater*, as well as the striking uniqueness in form and content, in compositional technique and structure of many of the other compositions, resulted in the fact that his art found its way into all parts of the world and that the name of its creator must be ranked amongst the greatest in the music of his time.

Nevertheless, the figure and personality of the Polish composer, the evolution of his work, and his struggle for the recognition he deserved, have remained largely unknown, mainly for lack of appropriate literature, particularly in foreign languages. This little book hopes to fill at least a modest part of the gap. It first appeared at a time when, on UNESCO's recommendation, the centenary of the composer's birth was being celebrated all over the world.

Stanislaw Golachowski (1907-1951), who wrote this book in 1948, was a musicologist of diverse talents. It is to him we owe the fact that the composer's documentary and biographical inheritance remained preserved to a considerable extent, despite all the devastations of World War II. As a result of Golachowski's early death, a monograph he had planned on Szymanowski was never completed.

Any details a non-Polish reader might have difficulty in understanding have been explained in the footnotes.

January 1982

The manuscript of Szymanowski's violin Concerto No. 2.

Music Examples

Prelude in C minor op. 1, no. 7 See text reference on p. 14

(1)

Theme & Variations in B flat minor See text reference on p. 14

(2)

Theme & Variations in B minor op. 10 See text reference on p. 16

Andantino semplice

The Swan op. 7 See text reference on p. 17

(4)

Lento maesto

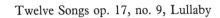

Twelve Songs op. 17, no. 9, Lullaby **See text reference on p. 17**

(5)

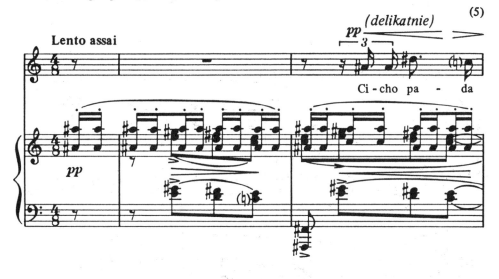

snieg   na piers pol   Wciaz na ser - ce pa - da mi snieg

2nd Symphony, 1st movement, main theme

See text reference on p. 21

(6)

Allegro moderato grazioso

skrz. I

P dolce espress.

dolce sf

poco rall.

a tempo

dolce   cre . . scen . . do   *poco f dolce*

2nd Piano Sonata, 1st movement, main theme

See text reference on p. 22

(7)

Allegro assai *(molto appassionato)*

The Love Songs of Hafiz op. 24, no. 2 See text reference on p. 30

(8)

3rd Symphony, violin part See text reference on p. 30

(9)

3rd Symphony, beginning of tenor solos See text reference on p. 30

(10)

Myths op. 30, no. 1, *Die Quelle der Arethusa*

(Poco allegro) meno mosso

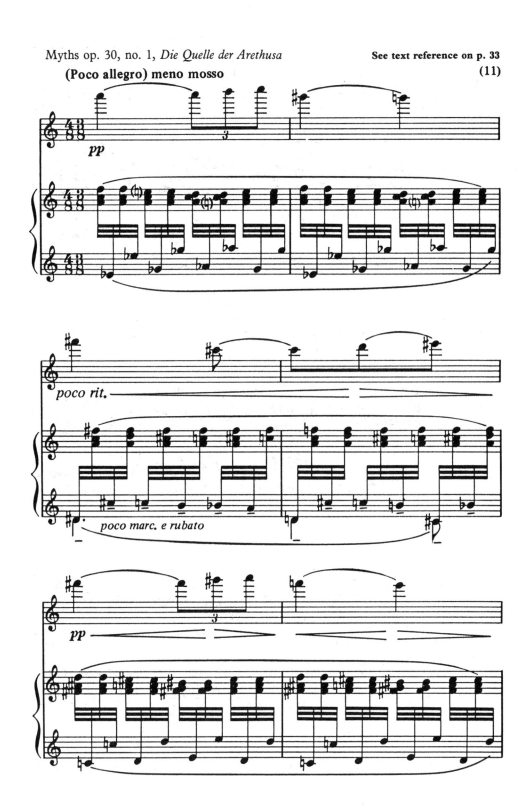

Masks op. 24, no. 1, *Sheherezade*

See text reference on p. 33

(12)

Lento assai Languido

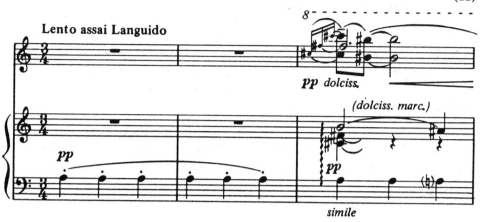

(Music example 12 continued)

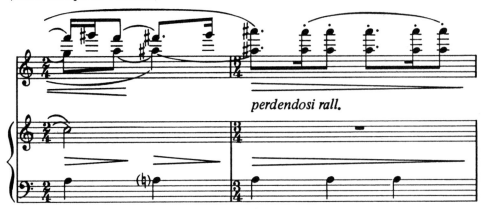

perdendosi rall.

1st Violin Concerto, beginning of violin solo

See text reference on p. 34
(13)

(Music example 13 continued)

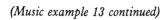

Third Piano Sonata

See text reference on p. 35

(14)

(Music example 14 continued)

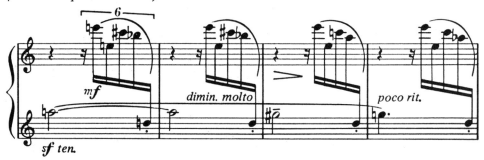

Songs of the Infatuated Muezzins op. 42, no. 1,
Allah, Allah, Akbar

See text reference on p. 38

(15)

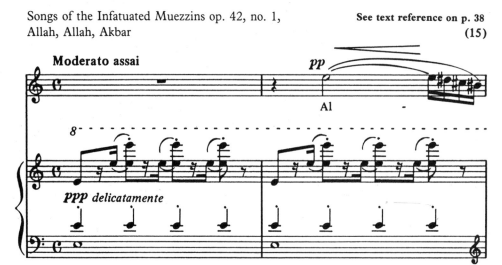

King Roger, 1st act, tenor solo, Shepherd's Song See text reference on p. 40

(16)

Slopiewnie op. 46, no. 2, *Grune Worte* See text reference on p. 41

(17)

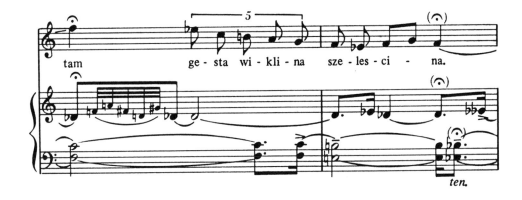

Harnasie, 2nd act, tenor solo

See text reference on p. 45
(18)

Tempo di marcia (ma animato)

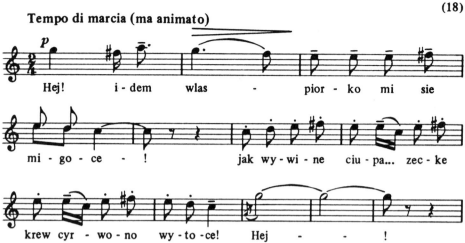

Hej! i - dem wlas - pior - ko mi sie

mi - go - ce - ! jak wy - wi - ne ciu - pa... zec - ke

krew cyr - wo - no wy - to - ce! Hej - !

Harnasie, 2nd act, wedding chorus

See text reference on p. 45
(19)

(allegramente)
Poco meno

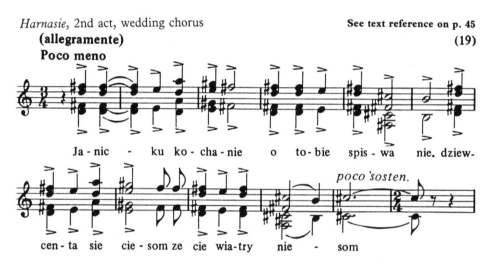

Ja - nic - ku ko - cha - nie o to - bie spis - wa nie. dziew-

poco sosten.

cen - ta sie cie - som ze cie wia - try nie - som

Harnasie, 3rd act, tenor solo

See text reference on p. 45
(20)

Poco meno mosso

Po - undz ze mi po - widz do us - ka pra - we - -

go - cy mnie ra da wi - dzis cy ko go in - ne go?

Mazurka op. 50, no. 9 See text reference on p. 46
(21)

Tempo moderato

Mazurka op. 50, no. 12 See text reference on p. 46
(22)

Allegro moderato

85

See text reference on p. 51

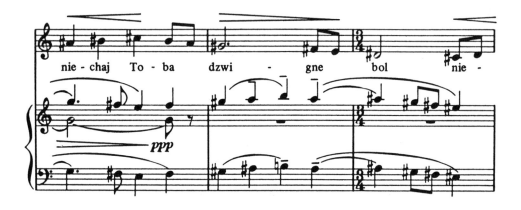

Stabat Mater, baritone solo

See text reference on p. 51
(24)

Children's Rhymes op. 49, no. 4, *Das Ferkelchen*

See text reference on p. 52
(25)

(*Music example 25 continued*)

See text reference on p. 63

Songs from *Kurpie* op. 58, no. 1, *Es Flogen Kraniche*

(26)

Le - cio - ty zo - ra - zie

krzy - ca - ty: moj Bo - ze, Ka - li - na zje-wo-rem

roz stac sie nie mo - ze

4th Symphony, 1st movement, main theme See text reference on p. 63

(27)

2nd Violin Concerto, beginning of violin solo See text reference on p. 64

(28)

A Brief Chronicle of the Composer's Life and Work

1882

Karol Szymanowski is born on October 3rd in Timoshovka as the son of Stanislaw Korwin-Szymanowski and Anna, née Taube.

1889

Aged 7, Karol receives the first piano lessons from his father. He continues the lessons (piano and theory) at the music school of Gustaw and Marta Neuhaus in Yelisavetgrad. His first attempts at composition date from this year.

1900

He passes the graduation examination at the grammar-school in Yelisavetgrad. Begins to compose, writes *Nine Preludes*, op. 1, for piano, starts *Six Songs*, op. 2, after poems by K. Tetmajer.

1901-1905

Szymanowski goes to Warsaw to study music. Takes lessons in harmony from M. Zawirski, in counterpoint and composition from Z. Noskowski. Becomes friendly with P. Kochanski, A. Rubinstein, and G. Fitelberg. In the fall of 1905 – under the patronage of Prince Lubomirski – Szymanowski, Fitelberg, Rozycki, and Szeluto establish the Publishing Syndicate of Young Polish Composers. From this period date the Variations in B flat minor, op. 3, *Four Etudes*, op. 4, and the Sonata in D minor, op. 9, for violin and piano.

1906-1908

On February 6th, 1906, the first concert by members of the Syndicate is given at the Warsaw Philharmonia. It includes, among other things, a performance of the Concert Overture in E major, op. 12, by Szymanowski. On March 30th, Fitelberg conducts a concert of music by young Polish composers in Berlin. Szymanowski makes several trips to Berlin and Leipzig. In 1907, members of the Syndicate give a concert in Warsaw which is very badly received by conservative critics. At the beginning of 1908, Szymanowski travels to Italy (to Nervi near Genoa).

1909-1911

The following pieces are produced: Symphony no. 2 in B flat major, op. 19; Piano Sonata no. 2, op. 21; *The Love Songs of Hafiz*, first cycle, op. 24; and other songs. In a competition for composers organized by the Lemberg Committee for the centenary celebrations of the birth of F. Chopin, Szymanowski wins first prize with his Piano Sonata no. 1, op. 8. Szymanowski makes two journeys to Italy. In 1910, he visits several cities, among them Rome, Florence, Venice, and in 1911 he goes to Sicily (Agrigento, Syracuse, Palermo). On April 7th, 1911, his Second Symphony has its premiere in Warsaw. Towards the end of the year, the composer moves to Vienna.

1913

First contact with the music of Stravinsky and the ballet company of Dyaghilev (*Petrushka* in Vienna). The composer spends the 1913/14 season in Zakopane.

1914

In March, he travels to Italy, then – via Sicily – to Africa (Constantine, Biskra, Tunis). On the return journey (via Rome, Paris, and London), he becomes acquainted with Stravinsky. Szymanowski's interest turns to ancient, oriental, and early Christian art. He composes a second cycle of *Hafiz Love Songs*, op. 26, for solo voice and orchestra, and begins work on his Symphony no. 3 ("Song of the Night"), op. 27.

1915-1916

The following piano works are composed: *Metopes*, op. 29, and *Masks*, op. 34. For violin: *Myths*, op. 30, and the Violin Concerto no. 1, op. 35. Further, the cycle *Songs of the Fairy Princess*, op. 31. Szymanowski makes several visits to Moscow and Petersburg.

1917-1918

As a consequence of the Revolution, the Szymanowski family moves from Timoshovka to Yelisavetgrad in the fall of 1917. Here the composer writes his novel *Ephebos* and discusses with J. Iwaszkiewicz plans for the opera *King Roger*. Composes the Piano Sonata, op. 36, the String Quartet no. 1, op. 37, *Songs of the Infatuated Muezzin*, op. 42. On December 24th, 1919 he arrives in Warsaw.

1920-1921

In March 1920, concerts of works by Szymanowski are organized in Cracow and Lemberg. The composer begins work on *King Roger*. Toward the end of the year, he travels via London to America. In England, he gets to know Dyaghilev; he counts on a commission for a ballet. During his stay in America, he visits Florida and Cuba. He spends the summer in Poland. In the fall, he embarks on his second trip to America. In letters to friends, he mentions ideas for a Gorale ballet. He composes the *Slopiewnie*, op. 46.

1922-1926

In spring of 1922 Szymanowski returns to Poland via Paris, where a triumphant concert of his works is given on May 26th. From August 1922, the composer frequently stays in Zakopane. He discusses plans for a ballet with M.J. Rytard. In September 1923, he starts to work on the ballet score. During the years 1924-25 he visits Paris on several occasions. The following works are produced: *Children's Rhymes*, op. 49; *20 Mazurkas*, op. 50; *Stabat Mater*, op. 53. The opera *King Roger* is completed. Its premiere takes place in Warsaw on June 19th, 1926.

1927-1929

In March 1927, Szymanowski takes up the post as director at the Warsaw Conservatory. Then follows the period of his teaching activity and his endeavors for a reform of musical education. The resulting battle with the conservative faculty undermines the composer's health. In 1928, Szymanowski goes to Edlach (Austria) to recuperate, and, in the summer of 1929, he hands in his resignation. In January 1929, his *Stabat Mater* has its premiere at the Warsaw Philharmonia. In March, the first scene of the ballet *Harnasie* is performed.

1930-1931

His treatment in Davos, which began towards the end of 1928, continues until

June 1930. In Davos he writes the pamphlet "The Educational Role of Musical Culture in Society." In November, at the beginning of the academic year, the opening ceremony takes place at the Warsaw Academy (formerly the Conservatory); Szymanowski becomes the Academy's first rector. In December, the Jagiello University in Cracow bestows an honorary doctorate upon him (the professor conferring the degree was Z. Jachimecki). The composer completes his work on the ballet *Harnasie*—its second scene is performed in May 1931. He begins work on the *Songs from Kurpie*, op. 58.

1932

In April Szymanowski resigns from his post as rector and moves to Zakopane. He works on the Symphony No. 4 (Sinfonia concertante), op. 60, and, after its completion, on the Violin Concerto no. 2, op. 61. In October a performance of *King Roger* is given at the Narodni Divadlo in Prague. In Poznan, the Symphony no. 4 is heard for the very first time, with the composer as soloist at the piano.

1933-1934

Severe financial hardship forces Szymanowski to go on numerous tours as a concert pianist. In November, he plays—among other places—in Moscow, then in Zagreb, Belgrade, Bucharest, Sofia, Paris, Amsterdam, The Hague, London, Glasgow, Copenhagen, Oslo, Riga, Bologna, and Rome.

1935-1936

Premiere of the ballet *Harnasie* in Prague on May 11th, 1935. On April 27th, 1936, the work is given its triumphant reception at the Grand Opera in Paris (the ballet being reorganized into three scenes). The composer spends the whole summer in Warsaw. His health, weakened by the strenuous travelling, grows rapidly worse. In December 1936, he goes to Grasse in Southern France.

1937

The composer, by now seriously ill, is taken to Cannes and shortly afterwards to a sanatorium in Lausanne, where he dies on March 29th, 1937 in the presence of his sister Stanislawa. The body of Karol Szymanowski is removed to Warsaw and buried on April 7th, 1937 in the Heroes' Crypt of St. Paul's Church on the Cracow "Skalka."

Works for the stage

Hagith, op. 25 (1912-1913), opera in one act, libretto after a tragedy by Felix Dörmann.

King Roger, op. 46 (1918-1924), opera in three acts, libretto by Jaroslaw Iwaszkiewicz and Karol Szymanowski.

Harnasie, op. 55 (1923-1931), ballet-pantomine in three acts after a scenario by Karol Szymanowski and Jerzy Mieczyslaw Rytard.

Mandragora, op. 43 (1920), pantomime in three scenes for symphony orchestra; grotesque ballet for the third act of the comedy *Le Bourgeois Gentilhomme* by Molière; scenario by Ryszard Boleslawski and Leon Schiller.

Prince Potemkin, op. 51 (1925), music to the fifth act of a tragedy by Tadeusz Micinski.

Men's Lottery (1908-1909), operetta in three acts.

Symphonic Works

Concert Overture in E major, op. 12 (1904-1905) for orchestra.

Symphony no. 1 in F minor, op. 15 (1906-1907) for orchestra.

Symphony no. 2 in B flat major, op. 19 (1909-1910) for orchestra.

Symphony no. 3 ("Song of the Night"), op. 27 (1916) for tenor or soprano, mixed choir and orchestra, after words by Jebal ad-Din Rumi.

Symphony no. 4 (Sinfonia concertante), op. 60 (1932) for piano and orchestra.

Vocal works with orchestra

Demetrius, op. 37 (1917), cantata for alto, female chorus, and orchestra, after words by Zofia Szymanowski.

Agave, op. 38 (1917), cantata for alto, female chorus, and orchestra, after words by Zofia Szymanowski.

Stabat Mater, op. 53 (1925-1926) for soprano, alto, baritone, mixed chorus, and orchestra, after the words of the Latin Sequence.

"Veni Creator," op. 57 (1930) for soprano, mixed chorus, organ, and orchestra, after words by Stanislaw Wyspianski.

Litany to the Virgin Mary, op. 59 (1930-1933), two fragments for soprano, female chorus, and orchestra, after words by Jerzy Liebert.

Penthesilea, op. 18 (1908), song for soprano and orchestra after words by Stanislaw Wyspianski.

The Love Songs of Hafiz, op. 26 (1914) for solo voice and orchestra after the Arabic texts as paraphrased by Hans Bethge.

Songs of the Fairy Princess, op. 31 (1933), for soprano and orchestra, after words by Zofia Szymanowski.

Songs of the Infatuated Muezzin, op. 42 (1934) for tenor (soprano) and orchestra, after words by Jaroslaw Iwaszkiewicz.

Slopiewnie, op. 46 (1928), songs for soprano and orchestra after words by Julian Tuwim.

Chamber Music

String Quartet no. 1 in C major, op. 37 (1917).

String Quartet no. 2, op. 56 (1927).

Piano Music

Nine Preludes, op. 1 (1899-1900).

Variations in B flat minor, op. 3 (1901-1903).

Variations on a Polish folk-theme in B minor, op. 10 (1900-1904).

Four Etudes, op. 4 (1900-1902).

Twelve Etudes, op. 33 (1916).

Fantasy in C major, op. 14 (1905).

Prelude and Fugue (1905, 1909).

Sonata no. 1 in C minor, op. 8 (1904).

Sonata no. 3 in A major, op. 21 (1910-1911).

Sonata no. 2, op. 36 (1917).

Metopes, op. 29 (1915).

Masks, op. 34 (1915-1916).

Twenty Mazurkas, op. 50 (1924-1926).

Four Polish Dances (1926).

Two Mazurkas, op. 62 (1933, 1934).

Romantic Waltz (1925).

Works for Violin and Piano

Sonata in D minor, op. 9 (1904).

Romance in D major, op. 23 (1910).

Nocturne and Tarantella, op. 28 (1915).

Myths, op. 30 (1915).

Three Paganini Capricci, op. 40 (1918).

"Berceuse d'Aïtacho Enia," op. 52 (1925).

Songs for Solo Voice and Piano

Six Songs, op. 2 (1900-1902), after words by Kazimierz Tetmajer.

Three Fragments, op. 5 (1902), after words by Jan Kasprowicz.

"The Swan," op. 7 (1904), after Waclaw Berent.

Four Songs, op. 11 (1904-1905), after words by Tadeusz Micinski.

Five Songs, op. 13 (1905-1907), after words by German poets.

Twelve Songs, op. 17 (1907), after words by German poets.

Six songs, op. 20 (1909), after words by Tadeusz Micinski.

A Medley of Songs, op. 22 (1910), after words by German poets.

The Love Songs of Hafiz, op. 24 (1911), after Arabic texts translated by Hans Bethge.

Songs of the Fairy Princess, op. 31 (1915), after words by Zofia Szymanowski.

Three Songs, op. 32 (1915), after words by Dmitri Dawydow.

Four Songs, op. 41 (1918), after words by Rabindranath Tagore.

Songs of the Infatuated Muezzin, op. 42 (1918), after words by Jaroslaw Iwaszkiewicz.

Slopiewnie, op. 46 et seq. (1921), after words by Julian Tuwim.

Three Lullabies, op. 48 (1922), after words by Jaroslaw Iwaszkiewicz.

Children's Rhymes, op. 49 (1922-1923), after words by Kazimiera Illakowiczowna.

Four Songs, op. 54 (1926), after words by James Joyce.

Twelve Songs from Kurpie, op. 58 (1930-1932), after folk-poetry.

Vocalise-Etude (1928).

Nine Polish Songs (1925-1926).

Choral Songs

Six Songs from Kurpie (1928) for mixed chorus *a cappella.*

The works of Karol Szymanowski were originally published by the following companies: Universal Edition (Vienna), Editions Max Eschig (Paris), and Polish Music Publishing Company (Cracow). At the time of this writing, an edition of the collected works of Karol Szymanowski, based on authentic sources, is in preparation. This edition is being prepared by the Polish Music Publishing Company in collaboration with the publishers listed above. Individual volumes may be ordered from:

ARS POLONA, Foreign Trade Enterprise, Krakowskie Przedmiescie 7, 00-068 Warszawa, Poland.

Universal Edition (London) Ltd., 2/3 Fareham Street, Dean Street, London, W. 1, England.

Universal Edition, Vertriebs-Ges. m. b. H., 1015 Wien, Postf. 130, Austria.

European American Music Distributors Corporation, 195 Allwood Road, P.O. Box 597, Clifton, N.J. 07012, U.S.A.

Editions Max Eschig, 48, Rue de Rome, Paris 8, France.

A detailed catalogue listing all of Szymanowski's works individually and stating where and when they were published, as well as supplying discographical data, is contained in the picture album *Szymanowski* by Teresa Chylinska. This volume was published in Polish by the Polish Music Publishing Company and in English by Twayne Publishers Inc., The Kosciuszko Foundation, New York.

Orders should be addressed to: ARS POLONA—Foreign Trade Office, Krakowskie Przedmiescie 7, 00-068 WARSZAWA, Poland and The Kosciuszko Foundation, 15 East 65th Street, NEW YORK, N.Y. 10020 U.S.A.

Index

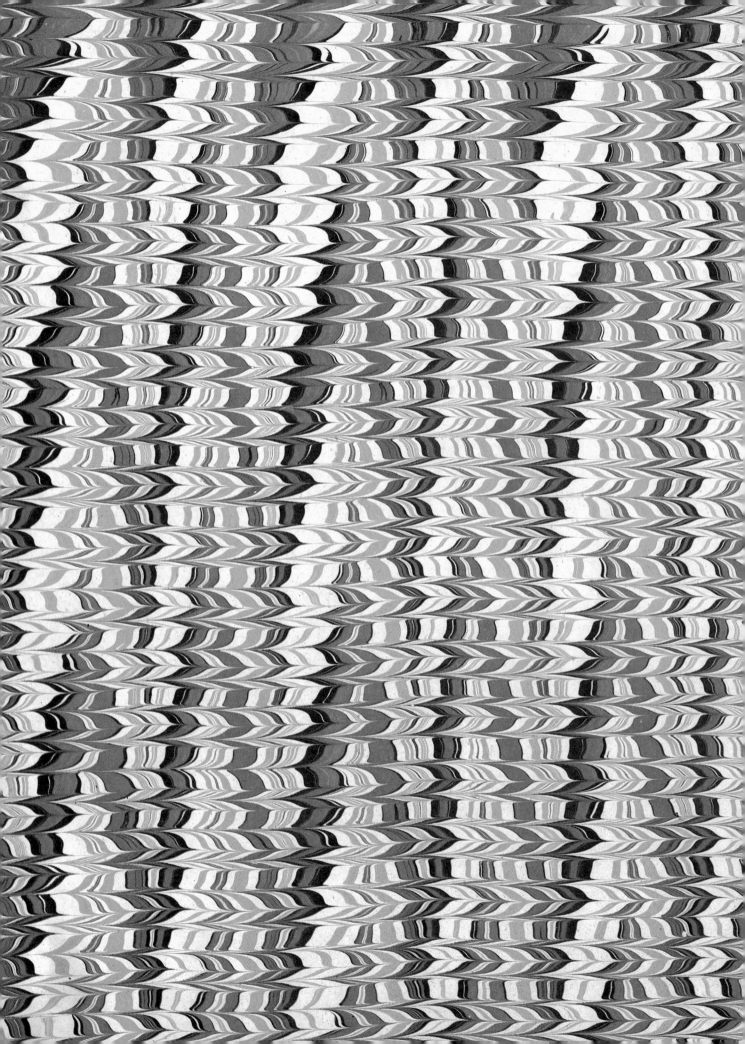